Secret Walks
Devon

Secret Walks
Devon

by Rob Smith
With additional texts by John Payne and Alex Whittleton

First published by *Secret Seeker*, an imprint of One More Grain Of Sand, 2016
info@onemoregrainofsand.com

www.secretseeker.com

Edited by Katie Halpin and Alex Whittleton
Research by Steve Marvell, Brendan Barry and Rob Smith
Photography by Brendan Barry, unless where stated below
Design by Ben Hoo, Nicola Erdpresser and Rob Smith
Maps by Dog's Body Design, Chunning Chang and Rob Smith
Printed by Cambrian Printers, Aberystwyth, Wales

ONE
MORE
GRAIN
OF
SAND

Photography credits: All photographs by Brendan Barry (www.brendanbarry.co.uk) except for the following. Pages 118–19 by ASC Photography; 50–51 by Pete Blackwell; 144–5 by Jon Combe; 152–3 David Hughes; 86–7 by John Longuet; 32 by Clive Ormonde; 94–5 by Alan Pewsey; 154 by Matt Roberts; 14-15, 22, 34-35, 42-43, 46-47, 48-49, 96-97, 100-101, 103, 104-105, 106-107, 132-133, 134, 147, 160 by Rob Smith; 40–41 by Rolf E Staerk; 58–9 by Chris Triggs; 136–7 by Joan Veale; 78–9 by David Wingate; 68–9 by Robert Wright.

ISBN: 978-1-910992-08-1

Help us update: More than two years, 1,000km and numerous pairs of walking shoes have gone into making this guide the best it can be, but if you think something could be improved, an instruction could be clearer or you find the perfect pitstop to include in the next edition, we'd love to hear from you: info@onemoregrainofsand.com

Publisher's note: Many of the walks within this publication follow steep, rocky pathways, which may be seldom used and susceptible to erosion. Every effort has been made to provide sufficient warning where necessary. The publisher and author accept no responsibility for injuries or deaths that arise from following the routes featured in this book. You are responsible for your own safety – rely on your own assessment of whether a particular route is suitable for your abilities and whether it has deteriorated since publication of the book to a point where it is not safe.

CONTENTS

INTRODUCTION

With its miles of surf-dashed coastline, the moody plateaus of Exmoor and Dartmoor, and the wood-wrapped river valleys of the South Hams, Devon is a magnet for lovers of the great outdoors. And there's no better way to seek out its most secluded, stunning parts than by pulling on your walking boots and exploring on foot.

It's said that if you walked every day for a year in Devon, you would never have to walk on the same path twice. And little wonder, in a county crisscrossed by around 5600km of walking trails and footpaths; 330km of these hug its beach-fringed shores as part of the spectacular South West Coast Path, while the rest traverse the high moors, rolling pastures and verdant valleys of inland Devon.

Whether you're a hiker or a stroller, fancy gently rolling countryside or rugged coastline, this guide will lead you to Devon's wildest, remotest, most breathtakingly beautiful parts. As you'll see, the county's lesser-known corners can be every bit as magnificent as its world-famous national parks and beaches. The guide also offers an insight into the history and culture of the county, in the form of Extra Step articles – one for each walk. We hope you enjoy every step.

THE COUNTRYSIDE CODE

RESPECT

When passing through farmland you should leave gates as you find them, either open or closed. Try to follow the paths and avoid straying over planted crops when you are in fields. Never block entrances to fields, driveways or paths with your car – always find a safe and unobtrusive place to park even if this means extending your walk by a few hundred metres.

PROTECT

Leave no trace of your visit and take your litter home. Keep dogs under close control at all times – a bad scare from a dog is enough to endanger the lives of valuable livestock. Always clear up dog mess and dispose of the collection bag or container properly.

ENJOY

Always plan ahead and be prepared for weather changes. Make sure you have enough daylight for the walk you are doing – with plenty of contingency time. Be sure to take note of any signage and warnings you see on the route.

HOW TO USE THIS BOOK

Important – read instructions carefully and stay on track
Devon is a fantastic place to explore on foot and the routes within this book
will take you to areas of the county that are wild and seldom trodden. At
regular intervals we ask you to look for small, specific markers in order to
find a pathway. This means you must be aware of your surroundings and
make sure you read the instruction you are following fully (and ideally the
subsequent one as well) in order to avoid getting lost. This is all the more
important when walking and chatting with friends and family – it is easy to
get distracted, misjudge distances and miss turnings.

Important for GPS users – estimated distances within the instructions
Rather than giving the exact distances recorded by GPS between reference
points in the instructions, we have given rough distances and adjusted them very
slightly according to the terrain. On rocky terrain it will always feel like you have
walked further than you actually have, and so we have accounted for this.

The walk durations are based on an easy pace of 3km/hr with no stopping time.

ICONS AND TECHNICAL INFORMATION

Each walk has a series of icons that will give you important information about
the route. Below is what they mean and how you should interpret them.

Max height

The maximum
height the walk
reaches above
sea level

**Total height
gain**

The total uphill
walking during
the walk

Walk difficulty

E = Easy
M = Medium
H = Hard
X = Extreme

Walk length

We have
rounded this
up to the
nearest 0.5km

Walk duration

This is based
on a pace of
3km/hr without
stops

**Walk addition
with optional
extras**

**Walk reduction
with shortcut
route**

**Panoramic views
rated 1 to 5**

**Family
suitability
rated 1 to 5**

**Nature and beauty
rated 1 to 5**

MAPS AND MAP KEY

The maps we have created for the book should be used to give you an idea of where you are along the route and a sense of your surroundings. It is not possible to show every road and pathway at the scale we use, so don't worry if you see turnings not marked on the map. Simply follow the detailed written instructions.

Walking route and instruction numbers

Optional extra or shortcut route

Wide asphalt road

Asphalt road or wide track

Track or pathway

Start and end point

Nature reserve

Church / chapel

Public or paid toilets

Archaeological site

Pitstop

Not to Miss location

Lighthouse

Castle

Picnic spot

Car park

Bird hide

Viewpoint

Swimming spot

GETTING THERE AND DISTANCES

In the Getting There instructions we have used miles as our measurement of distance because users will generally be driving to the start points. However, in the walk instructions, we have used kilometres as our unit of measurement. This is because walking is gradually moving over to the metric system. (You will notice that new signs on pathways use kilometres and metres as distance measurements.)

The postcodes in the Getting There instructions are for sat-nav devices and will take the user to the nearest marked postcode to the walk start point.

THE EXTRA STEPS

The Extra Step articles in this book cover a range of subjects that include nature, history, architecture and ethnography. These short, accessible essays complement each walk – we hope they will make your time exploring Devon even more enjoyable.

THE PITSTOPS

The Pitstops in each walk are places to stop for refreshment on or near the walking route. A selection of pubs, restaurants and cafés have been chosen and even some delis or shops where you can pick up supplies for a picnic.

WALK LENGTHS AND LOCATIONS

1   Heddon Valley
Hard – 13.5km
With optional extras – 15km
Shortcut walk distance – 8.5km

2   Muddiford & Marwood
Easy – 8km
No optional extras
No shortcut

3   Clovelly & Mouthmill
Easy/Medium – 6.5km
With optional extras – 8km
No shortcut

4   Roborough
Easy – 8km
No optional extras
Shortcut walk distance – 3.5km

5   Molland & Anstey Gate
Medium – 8km
No optional extras
Shortcut walk distance – 5.5km

6   Stoodleigh & Oakford
Medium – 10.5km
With optional extras – 11km
No shortcut

7   Cadeleigh & Bickleigh
Hard – 10km
With optional extras – 11.5km
Shortcut walk distance: #1 – 8.5km / #2 – 5km

8   Roadford Lake
Easy – 7.5km
No optional extras
No shortcut

9   Okehampton Station
Easy – 6.5km
No optional extras
Shortcut walk distance – 6km

10   Branscombe
Hard – 9km
With optional extras: #1 – 9.5km / #2 – 15km
Shortcut walk distance: #1 – 3.5km / #2 – 7km / #3 – 7.5km

11   Pullabrook Wood
Easy – 4.5km
No optional extras
No shortcut

12   Dartmoor Tors
Hard – 18.5km
No optional extras
No shortcut

13   Brent Moor
Hard – 11km
No optional extras
No shortcut

14   The Erme Estuary
Hard – 12km
No optional extras
No shortcut

15   Prawle Point
Medium/Hard – 13km
With optional extras – 18km
Shortcut walk distance: #1 – 5km / #2 – 9km

Lynton

Woolacombe

2

Barnstaple

Bideford

3

Hartland

Great
Torrington

4

5

6

Tiverton

Chulmleigh

7

Holsworthy

Hatherleigh

Crediton

Honiton

Okehampton

Exeter

Sidmouth

10

Seaton

8

9

Launceston

11

Newton
Abbot

12

13

Totnes

Plymouth

Dartmouth

14

Kingsbridge

15

241m | 481m | **H** | 13.5km | 4hrs | +1.5km | -5km

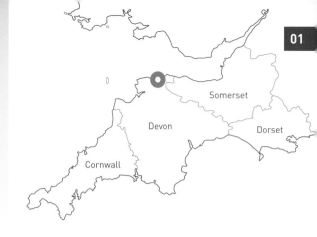

Somerset

Devon

Dorset

Cornwall

This route takes you over some of the highest and most dramatic cliffs on the South West Coast Path, from where – as you might expect – the views in all directions are sensational. On the inland stretch of the walk, you'll come to a superb pub before heading back to the start along the Tarka Trail – another long-distance footpath, which runs in a figure of eight across the North Devon countryside, past locations that feature in Henry Williamson's book *Tarka the Otter* (see p.33). If you can, follow the stream down through the lush, wooded river valley to the beach at Heddon's Mouth – you'll need a camera to capture the serene beauty of this spot, which was so favoured by the Romantic poets. This walk is fairly long and hard at times, so good footwear is essential. Be vigilant for landslides and take utmost care in strong winds.

N

400m
1,000ft

Ramsey
Beach

Elwill Bay

Heddon's
Mouth

Highveer
Point

The Cow
& Calf

Wringapeak

Woody Ba

50

100

Roman Fortlet

6

1

MARTINHOE

Sir Robert's Path

Slattenslade

TRENTISHOE

4

Trentishoe Hill

Trentishoe Lane

150

150

2

3

5

King's Lane

Slattenslad

Croscom
Bartor

Invention
Wood

200

South Dean Lane

150

8km

HEALE

KEMACOTT

Manacott Lane

Jose's Lane

Berry's Ground Lane

Cherry Tor Lane

Martinhoe
Common

250

Heale Down Lane

200

150

Broadoak Hill

200

250

200

Higher
Cowley

Gratton Lane

250

Wheatly Lane

Cowley Wood Hill

PARRACOMBE

Parracombe Lane

Parracombe
Lane Head

Church Lane

A39

250

A39 Long Lane

150

250

CLIMBS

Pencombe Rocks

225m
200m
175m
150m
125m
100m
75m
50m

2km   4km   6km   8km   10km   12km   14km

GETTING THERE

Locate Berry's Ground Lane near Martinhoe – it should be marked on most maps. Turn left onto Sir Robert's Path and follow it downhill, around a sharp right-hand bend. Park in the large parking bay on the right. EX31 4QX.

WALK DIRECTIONS

1 Follow the road down the hill and after a few metres, turn left onto a narrow lane, downhill again, signposted Wringapeak. Walk about 500m to the sharp right-hand bend and fork off onto the track ahead – this is the coast path. Follow it out to the cliff path and keep going, without diverting onto lesser paths, for about 2.5km. The path will veer inland along the side of the impressive Heddon Valley, where you will get your first impression of this steep, deep natural phenomenon. Keep going as you descend and eventually you reach a T-junction.

OPTIONAL EXTRA – To take an optional route to Heddon's Mouth beach, turn right at the T-junction and follow your nose down to the beach and back.

2 To continue the route, turn left at the T-junction, following the sign to our first Pitstop, the Hunters Inn (see p.23), and walk about 250m to the footbridge. This is where our shortcut starts. But, to continue the route, turn right to cross over the footbridge and follow signs for the coast path – to get there, you take a left after 150m, then a right after 250m.

SHORTCUT – When you arrive at the footbridge, do not cross over; simply follow the wide and well-established riverside pathway straight ahead and all the way to the Hunters Inn and pick up the route from Instruction 5. (If the riverside path is boggy and muddy after lots of rain, you can follow the left fork on the surfaced path.)

3 Once on the coast path, simply follow it for about 2km to a junction with a left turn (after 1km, ignore the left turn to Trentishoe Church). This turn is signposted as a Permitted Path to a 'Country Road'. Take this path inland across the field to the lane.

4 Turn left onto the lane, then immediately right to walk downhill on another lane. Walk past the farm and cottages to a T-junction. Go straight ahead onto a narrower lane and then fork left straight away onto a pathway signposted Black Cleave. This takes you down a steep hill for a few hundred metres to a pathway junction. Turn left and follow the path to a lane (keeping the river on your right). At the lane, turn right and follow road signs for 500m to the Hunters Inn.

5 Continuing the route past The Hunters Inn (which will be on your left), just after the main pub building, turn left to walk uphill a few metres and then fork left onto a well-surfaced path signposted Woody Bay. (The shortcut arrives here – but it's best to orientate yourself outside the pub on the road and follow from the beginning of this instruction.) After 100m, fork right and join the higher path, then follow this main track for 2km – at which point you'll see a small path and sign for the Roman fortlet on your right (see opposite). Continuing the route past the fortlet, stay on the main track and you'll eventually arrive at a gate.

6 From the gate, follow the track straight ahead for about 1km, until you reach a lane. You should recognise this as Sir Robert's Path from your drive to the start point. Turn left and follow it downhill the short distance to the parking area, where you started the walk.

NOT TO MISS

Roman fortlet

This small, round, 1st-century AD fort is thought to have been occupied by a garrison of 80 Roman soldiers. Built to keep an eye on the Welsh across the Channel, it offers superb 360-degree views. Its boundaries are still visible today. (SS663493)

THE PITSTOPS

The Hunters Inn

After the challenges of a clifftop walk, you'll be pleased to find this B&B, with its excellent restaurant and bar. Stop off here for a plate of hearty food and a pint of home-brew by the fire, and – if you fancy it – you can stay overnight. Well-behaved dogs are welcome. Heddon Valley, Exmoor EX31 4PY. Open daily noon–3, 6–9 01598 763230. www.thehuntersinnexmoor.co.uk

Ye Olde George and Dragon

This 400-year-old inn comprises a lively bar and family-friendly restaurant, where plenty of games keep everyone amused before the food arrives. Sunday lunch is popular, so book ahead. Castle St, Combe Martin EX34 0HX. Open Mon–Fri 4–late, Sat & Sun noon–late. 01271 882282. www.georgeanddragon.uk.com

THE EXTRA STEP

Exmoor in literature

Exmoor is not for the faint-hearted. A high desolate plain with a treeless heartland, towering coastal cliffs and rolling sea mists, it can be a forbidding place at times. But it's this stark beauty that lends the moor its enduring appeal, enthralling everyone from the Romantic poets to modern-day lovers of the great outdoors. And nowhere is the moor's wild and weatherworn character more palpable than in the Heddon Valley, the setting for this walk, which swoops down dramatically from the heather and bracken of the high moor to the wild tidal races of the Bristol Channel at Heddon's Mouth. It's little wonder the Romantics were drawn here, with their sense of the sublime in nature.

Both William and Mary Wordsworth fell in love with the moor, where they spent long periods, and Samuel Taylor Coleridge settled with his family for a number of years in the Quantock Hills, the distinctive outliers of Exmoor to be found on the Somerset side of the border. The idea for his epic poem *The Rime of the Ancient Mariner* came to him while out on a walk with the Wordsworths in 1797 between Nether Stowey, a few kilometres east of the moor, and Dulverton to the south. The moor was also where he composed the magical *Kubla Khan* and began working on the *Lyrical Ballads* with Wordsworth, which is considered to mark the beginning of the Romantic movement in England. You can visit Coleridge's dark, low-ceilinged cottage, now owned by the National Trust, in the village of Nether Stowey.

But it wasn't just the Romantics who were struck by the untamed beauty of Exmoor; indeed, the landscape forms the remote, romantic backdrop to RD Blackmore's famous 1869 novel, *Lorna Doone*. The story is set in the late 17th century, during the turbulent years of the Monmouth Rebellion – an uprising led by the Duke of Monmouth, a Protestant, who wanted to overthrow Catholic King James II. It tells a tale of love between the young farmer Jan Ridd and the eponymous Lorna Doone, which has continued to intrigue visitors for well over a century. As Henry Williamson (see p.33), of *Tarka the Otter* fame, once wrote: 'There are three things read more or less regularly in the large outlying district of the moor – *Holy Bible*, *The News of the World*, and *Lorna Doone*. The Bible supplies the spiritual needs, the newspaper supplies the human interest, and Lorna Doone supplies the summer flow of visitors.'

Exmoor is a place that stirs the soul. Whatever the weather and whatever the time of year, nature always puts on a show here. And although the area is prone to extreme weather, as the devastating 1952 flood in the village of Lynmouth so vividly attests, more often than not, you'll see its more majestic side – its gently undulating combes, its teeming wildlife and, in summer, its swathes of brightly coloured wildflowers.

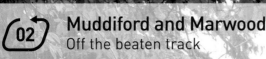
 159m
 309m
 E
 8km
 2.5hrs

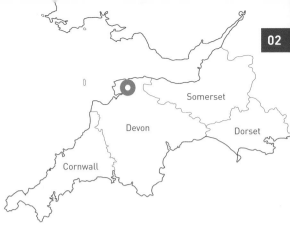

Somerset

Devon

Dorset

Cornwall

You'd be wise to find a beating stick on this route through lush countryside and farmland, because it includes a short section that can get quite overgrown in the summer. For most people, forging a path down these hidden tracks is a welcome excitement on what is, otherwise, a relatively easy-going walk. But fear not if a bit of bushwhacking is not your thing – there's an easier alternative. The route also contains one or two steep climbs, for which you'll be rewarded with magnificent countryside views. Otherwise, diversions include a popular tearoom set in stunning private gardens and an ancient pub that played a pivotal role in local life during World War II. So expect plenty of opportunity for rest, relaxation and refreshment after your exertions.

Metcombe

Swindon Down

Whitefield Barton

Middle Marwood

Gipsy Corner

Raised Path

Whiddon

Milltown

B3230

4

3

2

Whiddon Lane

5

Higher Muddiford

6

1

MUDDIFORD

Whitefield Barton

9

Whitehall Mill

Marwood Hill Gardens

Marwood

7

Guineaford

8

Kingsheanton

Prixford

North Lane

Whitefield Hill

Rookbear Lane

Shirwell R

N

400m
1,000ft

Blakewell

Tutshill

ASHFORD

CLIMBS

170m
150m
130m
110m
90m
70m

1km 2km 3km 4km 5km 6km 7km 8km

GETTING THERE

Muddiford is a village centred on the B3230, just north of Barnstaple. The walk starts at the car park of our first Pitstop, the Muddiford Inn (see p.31), which is easily found next to the main road. Be sure to ask permission from the landlord, with the promise of your business after the walk. EX31 4HA.

WALK DIRECTIONS

1 Walk out of the car park and turn left onto the road. After 50m or so, you reach a small church; turn left onto the lane just after it, walk over the bridge and, after about 100m, turn right onto the track – signposted as a footpath. Follow the arrows and the path roughly along the stream valley for about 750m. You will go through several gates and have to follow your nose where the path is indistinct but, eventually, you will reach a field that's directly opposite a house – it's about halfway up the left-hand bank of the valley. Walk over to the gate near the house, go along the short driveway (public access) and then follow a lane straight ahead, past several houses, for about 150m, until you reach another lane.

2 Cross over the lane into the field opposite and go straight ahead and over the stream into the next field, where you will have a steep hill on your left. Walk up the hill towards the large gap in the trees at the top. Just as you crest the brow of the hill, you'll see a footpath sign over to the right. Follow this short path through to a lane.

NOT TO MISS

Marwood Hill Gardens

This peaceful private garden, which was established in the late 1950s, is known for its lakes, hothouses and diverse collection of plants, fruit trees and shrubs. Don't miss the plant-sale area, where you'll find all kinds of weird and wonderful greenery to take home with you, and the excellent tearoom – our second Pitstop (see p.31) – which boasts fantastic views across the valley. Marwood, Barnstaple EX31 4EB. Open Mar–Sep 10–5; times vary out of season. 01271 342528. www.marwoodhillgarden.co.uk

3 Turn left onto the lane and walk around a bend, then uphill. After only 50m, turn onto a footpath on the left and walk straight ahead across the field. Go through the left-hand gate when you reach it and walk straight ahead through the farm and past the cottages to the lane.

4 Turn left onto the lane and walk downhill, and then follow the footpath sign to the right at the bend in the road. You will walk along a farm track, through another farm, and then through the middle of a field to another lane. Go straight over into the field opposite and walk straight ahead up the slight hill. When you reach the brow of the hill, walk over to the footpath sign, which is diagonally to your left.

5 At the sign you will find a bridleway that's raised higher than the surrounding fields. In winter, it should be easily passable, but if it is overgrown then go through into the field on the left and walk along the field edge (just next to the bridleway). Taking either route, you will arrive at a gate that leads onto a farm track. Turn left onto this pretty track, which is lined with bluebells and primroses in spring. Eventually, you will reach an asphalt lane.

6 Turn left onto the lane and walk past several houses. After about 500m, turn left onto a pathway. Walk diagonally right across the field to the far left (top) corner. In the next field, follow the left-hand field edge, then join the track to walk past the farm buildings and then walk uphill on the lane, past the church and into Marwood.

7 After the church, turn right at the junction and you'll see the entrance to Marwood Hill Gardens (see p.29), which has a tearoom (see opposite), on your right. Keep going on the lane. After 150m, you will pass the village hall and then, after a further 200m, you will arrive at a crossroads. This is the pretty village of Guineaford. Go straight over at the crossroads and continue for 500m or so until you arrive in the village of Kings Heanton.

8 In Kings Heanton, keep following the lane around a few bends and past houses until you reach a sharp right-hand bend, where you will see the village notice board. Follow the road straight ahead here, instead of going round the bend. You will walk past several more houses and then the lane will turn into a track and bridleway. Follow for about 250m and then turn left to keep following. After another 250m, turn right then, after a third 250m section, turn left onto the pathway into a field. Follow the left-hand field edge straight ahead and join the track in the far left corner. Veer left towards a lane.

9 Turn right onto the lane and follow it down the hill. You will recognise where you turned off at the start. Walk past the church and turn right to follow the main road 50m back to the Muddiford Inn.

THE PITSTOPS

The Muddiford Inn

This 16th-century coaching inn has had a fascinating history, particularly during World War II, when it was used as a restaurant for servicemen and -women. Today, the vibrant establishment at the heart of the community serves great value, generous meals. Muddiford, Barnstaple EX1 4EY. Open Tue–Thu noon–2.30 & 4–11, Fri & Sat noon–midnight, Sun noon–10.30. 01271 850243 www.themuddifordinn.co.uk

The Garden Tea Room

Enjoy a seasonally changing menu of light meals in the tearoom or blossom-filled tea garden at Marwood Hill Gardens (see p.29). Marwood, Barnstaple EX31 4EB. Open Mar–Sep 10–4.30; times vary out of season. 01271 342528. www.marwoodhillgarden.co.uk

THE EXTRA STEP

Historic Barnstaple

Barnstaple's position on the north bank of the Taw-Torridge estuary – a wide expanse of water flowing out into the Bristol Channel, to the south of this walk – led to its centuries-long status as one of the foremost river ports in Britain. From the Middle Ages to the 18th century, when the harbour silted up, the town was a major exporter of wool. After that, it became a thriving centre for industry, with shipbuilders, potteries, foundries, tanneries, sawmills and manufacturers of lace, sails and fishing nets springing up all over town.

Remnants of this rich history can be seen in the town centre, where the 19th century has left a particularly vivid mark. The Pannier Market, which was built in 1855, is a quintessential building of the Victorian railway age. It has a long hall and central nave of iron columns and girders, with high windows that infuse the bustling scenes below with natural light. The market is open six days a week throughout most of the year: on Tuesdays, Fridays and Saturdays, expect a general market, selling locally grown fruit, vegetables, plants, flowers, clothes, shoes, books, bric-a-brac, and arts and crafts; on Mondays and Thursdays, there's a focus on crafts, and on Wednesdays, antiques and collectables. If your visit coincides with the popular Friday market, take a moment to contemplate that its roots go back a staggering 800 years.

After you've visited the Pannier Market, be sure to stop by at neighbouring Butcher's Row, which was built at around the same time and in the same style, as well as the High Street, where several buildings have fine Victorian façades that hide even earlier interiors. Although Barnstaple's original Victorian station, on the south bank of the river, has been replaced by a rather bleak platform on an industrial estate, the journey there, across the medieval Barnstaple Long Bridge, is like walking back in time. This Grade I-listed bridge has been restored many times over the centuries, and the locals insist that every one of its 16 arches is different.

But that's not all in the way of history in this ancient town, which is thought to be one of the oldest boroughs in the country. There's also a fine museum, which comprises a regimental collection of the Royal Devon Yeomanry (formed in 1920) and celebrates local author Henry Williamson's much-loved 1927 novel, *Tarka the Otter*, which is set in and around the nearby rivers Taw and Torridge. For families after a more immersive experience, the nearby Heritage Centre is ideal, with its hands-on exhibits that show what life was like in the town from late-Saxon times to the genteel 18th century.

194m

289m

E/M

6.5km

2.5hrs

+1.5km

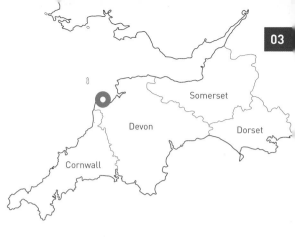

Somerset

Devon

Dorset

Cornwall

This delightful walk will lead you through a coastal country estate and along a stretch of dramatic coast path with jaw-dropping views over Bideford Bay. At about the halfway point, you'll come to pretty Mouthmill beach, with its jutting rock formations and large swathes of golden sand – the perfect place to stop for a picnic lunch and gaze out across the bay. This is an easy-going walk with only one steep descent, which veers off the main coast path and requires stout footwear. Gorgeous all year round, the route is particularly lovely in the springtime, when vivid carpets of bluebells pop up across the woodland floors.

Blackchurch Rock

Mouthmill Beach

The Cave

Brownsham Wood

Gallantry Bower

Snaxland Wood

Angel's Wings

Rushbush Copse

West Wood

Winsley Wood

Sheltered Seat

Court Farm

Clovelly Court

CLOVELLY

WRINKLEBERRY

Wrinkleberry Lane

HUGGLEPIT

Velly Wood

Burscott

B3237

B3248

N

400m
1,000ft

50
100
50
100
100
100
100
150
150

1
2
3
4
5
6
7

CLIMBS

Elevation profile: 200m, 175m, 150m, 125m, 100m, 75m, 50m
1km, 2km, 3km, 4km, 5km, 6km

HIGHER CLOVELLY

GETTING THERE

Take the A39 towards Clovelly, turning off at Clovelly Cross Filling Station, passing through Higher Clovelly, to Clovelly Court. Use the small parking area at the blue gates on a sweeping right bend, at the entrance to Clovelly Court Gardens. EX39 5SY. There's more parking a bit further along the road on the right, just after the right-hand bend mentioned in Instruction 1.

WALK DIRECTIONS

1 Carry on down the road on foot and after about 300m, just on the right-hand bend, go through the gate and down the pathway. After 25m, turn right onto the main path.

2 Walk along to the gate, which you pass through and turn left. This is now the coast path. Follow it as it curves to the right and into woods, keeping the sea on your right, until you reach a metal kissing gate. Go through this and along the right-hand field edge, and then through a wooden gate and into woods once more. You will walk past a sheltered seat, go down the steps and follow left. Now go through several kissing gates and sections of woodland, and along right-hand field borders for about 2km. You will reach a second sheltered seat called Angel's Wings.

NOT TO MISS

Angel's Wings

Sir James Hamlyn Williams, a former owner of Clovelly Court, built this wooden shelter in the 19th century so that he could sit in this spot and look across Bideford Bay to Youlston Park, where his daughter lived. The shelter was decorated with elaborate carvings of angels' wings by a former butler at Clovelly Court. (SS309257)

3 150m or so after Angel's Wings, make sure you take the right fork to stay on the coast path. Go through the field on the clear path, then down the hill to a well-defined junction. Here, you have an optional extra to two spectacular viewpoints (see below). To continue the route, follow the signs for the coast path down to Mouthmill beach.

OPTIONAL EXTRA – Turn right at the junction mentioned in Instruction 3 onto the Permissive Path. Then, after 250m, just before the small summerhouse, turn right onto a smaller path to find The Cave (see p.39). After the cave, walk past the summerhouse to reach a second viewpoint.

ALTERNATIVE HARD ROUTE – From the second viewpoint, there is a path leading to the left and down a steep section of headland. This is a hard (and slippery) alternative to walking back to rejoin the coast path. It leads you down to the small plateau in Instruction 4.

4 Taking the easy route and staying on the coast path (or walking back the short distance from the viewpoint optional extra), head down the hill to Mouthmill beach. You will arrive at a small plateau just above the beach. To continue the route without visiting the beach, turn left and follow the wide track inland past the cottage.

OPTIONAL EXTRA – To access Mouthmill beach, either look for the small steep path just by the plateau edge or go along and over the bridge. Be sure to admire the impressive Blackchurch Rock – looking very much like a church spire, as its name suggests, it's easy to imagine why this is used as a navigational aid, even today, for ships out at sea. Take care when exploring its interior – the rock surfaces can be very slippery.

5 Continuing the route inland past the cottage, turn right after 500m, cross the small river and then turn right again. Walk around the edge of the woods and, after a further 500m or more, look for the rocky bridleway that leads uphill to the left – it cuts back on you slightly.

6 Turn onto the bridleway and walk up to the bridle gate. Go through this and follow the left-hand field edge. In the next field, walk diagonally uphill to the far right-hand corner. Go through the gate and left onto the track.

7 Now simply follow the track, which leads over cattle grids, through Court Farm, past pretty meadows and all the way back to Clovelly Court. When you reach the wide driveway here, turn right and find your car at the start point. If you parked at the alternative parking, turn left on the road and walk 300m to find the right turn for the car park.

NOT TO MISS

Clovelly Court Gardens

Vegetables, herbs and fruit, including chillis, apricots and figs, are grown in this Victorian kitchen garden. The adjacent All Saints church boasts Norman porch carvings, fragments of ancient stained glass and five granite pillars that were transported by some unknown means from Lundy Island around 600 years ago. Outside, you'll find the gravestones of large local families, many of which still have descendants in the village. Clovelly Court is a private residence. Open daily 10–4. 01237 431200
www.clovelly.co.uk/village/clovelly-court-gardens

NOT TO MISS

The Cave

This hidden archway, which leads through the cliff, is a
little-known but spectacular feature – when you clamber
through it, expect to see panoramic views over Clovelly to
Bideford Bay beyond. (SS300264)

THE PITSTOPS

The Cottage Tea Rooms

This traditional tearoom has wooden tables, quirky teapots and
a characterful owner. Enjoy the sea views as you tuck into your
Devon cream tea from the courtyard. Admission charge for village.
High St, Clovelly, Bideford EX39 5TQ. Open Easter–Nov daily 10–6
01237 431494. www.clovelly.co.uk/map/cottage-tea-rooms

The Red Lion Hotel

This quaint hotel occupies an enviable position down on Clovelly's
harbour. Expect fish landed just outside the door and produce from
Clovelly Court Gardens (see opposite). Admission charge for village.
48 The Quay, Clovelly, Bideford EX39 5FT. Open daily noon–2.30 &
6–8.30. 01237 431237. www.stayatclovelly.co.uk/red-lion

THE EXTRA STEP

Charles Kingsley and local tourism

The seafaring tradition of this part of the North Devon coast was built around the sheltered ports of Bideford, at the head of the Torridge estuary, and Barnstaple, on the Taw estuary. Not only were these communities important trading ports, but they also supplied sailors – both willing and coerced – to the Royal Navy, which had the job of expanding the British Empire.

It was the area's rich maritime history that inspired the English academic and clergyman Charles Kingsley, who grew up in nearby Clovelly, to write his bestselling novel of 1855, *Westward Ho!*. A tale of adventure on the high seas set during Elizabethan times, the story moves between Bideford and the Caribbean, and was a roaring success in its day. As interest in this stretch of coastline grew as a result of the novel, speculators saw an opportunity to develop a long strip of sandy beach directly north of Bideford into a resort for tourists, naming it after Kingsley's novel. But visitors didn't think much of the new town: in 1899, the English poet and novelist Rudyard Kipling described it as 'twelve bleak houses by the shore'. To the surprise of many, however, Westward Ho! still exists today. Despite its rather unsightly hotchpotch of architectural styles, it's a popular tourist destination, particularly with watersports enthusiasts. It remains the only English town to have been named after a novel and to include an exclamation mark in its name.

Also put on the map by Kingsley's famous novel was the author's childhood home of Clovelly, a picture-postcard place that feels more like an open-air museum than a real community. Unusually, the village is privately owned, so cars are not allowed on the single, steep cobbled street here (known as 'Up-along' or 'Down-along' by the locals, depending on which way you're moving); instead, they must be left at the visitor centre, where you pay an entrance fee to the village, which includes access to its two museums. If you can see past the droves of tourists on the main street or if you visit in the off-season, you'll catch a glimpse of the quaint, flower-bedecked wattle-and-daub cottages that line the high street and the sledges that replaced donkeys in the last century to haul supplies around the town. Clovelly was, for centuries, one of the most important fishing villages on this stretch of coast, although evidence of this once-thriving industry is scant down at its tiny, tranquil harbour these days.

 173m

 236m

 E

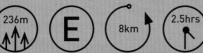 8km

2.5hrs

-4.5km

As the sub-title suggests, this walk is one for lovers of ale and a good, hearty meal in a cosy local inn. Furthermore, the route we've chosen to accompany this countryside 'pub crawl' is perfectly suited – it's not too long or strenuous, and includes some superb views to ensure you keep a gentle pace. We even offer an incredibly economical shortcut for anyone in favour of more time in the pub than on foot! Taking a circular route between the villages of Roborough and Beaford, you'll pass through several leafy valleys, follow woodland trails and trot along sleepy country lanes. The pub at the start and end of the walk, the New Inn (see p.49), is – in our humble opinion – one of the best in Devon. The Globe Inn, found halfway around the route, has friendly staff and is the perfect place to take a break from the walk.

ROBOROUGH

Wansley
Barton

Whitsley
Barton

Lower
Whitsleigh

12

Coombe Wood

Owlacombe

2

11

Great
Barlington

Middle
Barlington

10

Trigger's Hill

3

9
8

7

6

Upcott Barton

4

Lower
Upcott

Do
Fa

5

BEAFORD

Coombe
Farm

Beafo
Moo

A3124

CLIMBS

170m
150m
130m
110m
90m

1km 2km 3km 4km 5km 6km 7km 8km

GETTING THERE

Roborough is located about 3 miles east of Great Torrington, just north of the A3124. In the village, park on the wide part of the road near the church or at the New Inn, our first Pitstop (see p.49). EX19 8SY.

WALK DIRECTIONS

1 Find your way to the New Inn, which is on a corner in the centre of the village. Standing on the road that runs directly through the centre of the village and with your back to the pub, turn left and walk towards the church tower, which you should see above the rooftops ahead of you. After less than 50m, turn right onto a small lane to walk downhill. Keep on the lane for 750m and, just after some woodland encloses the lane, turn left onto a woodland pathway. Follow this downhill and let it lead you to the right and along the pretty valley.

2 After 250m or so, you arrive at a lane. The shortcut starts here (see below). Turn left, walk over the stream and then join the path going up the steep field ahead of you – walk towards the farm buildings at the top and then veer right to follow the left-hand field edge until you reach a gate. Go through the gate and turn left onto the concrete farm track. After a few metres, follow the farm track around to the right between buildings. This is Great Barlington. Make sure you fork right to stay on the concrete track across a field.

SHORTCUT – This reduces the walk length to about 3.5km – perfect for anyone in need of a thirst-quencher or satisfying meal at the excellent New Inn in Roborough. Simply turn left when you meet the lane, walk over the stream and follow the lane around to the right. Keep to the lane for about 400m and, when you see a turning onto a lane on the right ahead of you, look for the bridleway on the right. Turn onto it and go over the footbridge. Now simply skip to Instruction 10, where the footbridge is mentioned.

3 The track takes you to a gate and, immediately after, another gate on the left. Go through both and follow the footpath arrow directly across the field ahead of you. You will walk downhill to a stream. Go over into the next field and walk diagonally right, through the gap, then uphill on the same bearing to the next stile. Go over into the next field and walk along the right-hand edge to the back of some farm buildings, where you should find a stile leading over to a farm track.

4 Turn right onto the farm track and then go straight ahead to leave Upcott Barton farm behind you. Follow past a house, down into a valley, over a stream and uphill towards Beaford. As you near the village, make sure you turn right onto a pathway that takes you across a field. Go through a kissing gate and walk ahead on the lane to the road.

5 Turn right, walk past our second Pitstop, the Globe Inn (see p.49) – or pop in for a rest and refreshments – and after about 50m further on, turn down the narrow lane (more of a track). You should see a faded footpath sign just on the corner. Follow this downhill and let it lead you left. You will find yourself following a small stream on what is known as a 'green lane'. Keep following this all the way to an asphalt lane.

6 At the asphalt lane, turn right, go over the bridge, go over the stile on the left and then into a field. Walk diagonally uphill, roughly in the direction of a telegraph pole. From the telegraph pole, walk slightly right to the gate and you should see a post with a yellow arrow on it. In the next field, follow the direction of the yellow arrow to a gate leading into a third field. Here, you should follow the worn pathway along the right-hand edge.

7 After 50m, turn downhill to the left, walk along the bottom field edge and look carefully for an overgrown pathway sign and a gate next to the stream. It can be difficult to find, especially in summer when the vegetation is high. (The signpost is located within a patch of vegetation and the gate on the other side of the patch is in the field border itself.)

8 Go through the gate, over a stile and then over the stream on stepping stones, which are located about 20m over to the left.

9 Having crossed the stream, walk uphill along the right-hand field edge, go through the gap when you meet it and continue uphill in the next field, along the left-hand edge. Walk over the top of the hill and down towards Middle Barlington farm.

10 Just before the first building, fork right onto a muddy track and straight across the small field ahead. Turn left and walk along the field edge to the bottom right-hand corner, where there is a stile. Go over it to a lane.

11 Turn right onto the lane and follow for about 1km. You will see a bridleway on the left about 50m after a steep section and a left turn. Join the bridleway, go over the footbridge and follow the main track for 100m to a junction. You are now in Coombe Wood. Turn right at the junction, go through the gate and turn left at the crossways after a few metres. Go straight ahead at the next crossways, after 250m. After a further 250m, the track will have turned into a pathway. Ignore the small path on the right and keep going to walk past a house.

12 After the house, the path turns sharply to the right. Follow along to the track, which is also the driveway for the house. Turn left onto this and, after 250m, you will go through a gate and arrive at a lane. Turn left onto the lane and you will soon recognise it as the lane you walked along at the start. Follow your footsteps back to Roborough.

THE PITSTOPS

The New Inn

The menu at this 16th-century thatched pub is filled with typical
pub dishes done superbly well – think local, rare-breed sausage
and mash and ale-battered local fish with chips and peas. The pub
supports local breweries and cider-makers, too.

Roborough EX19 8SY. Open Mon & Tue 5–11, Wed noon–3 & 5–11,
Fri–Sun noon–11. 01805 603247. www.thenewinnroborough.co.uk

The Globe Inn

Expect slap-up meals and real ales at this pub. Muddy boots and
dogs are welcome – convenient, given it's halfway around our route.

Beaford EX19 8LR. Open Tue–Fri noon–3 & 5.30–11, Sat noon–11,
Sun noon–4. 01805 603358. www.globeinnbeaford.co.uk

THE EXTRA STEP

A love story

This walk lies close to the beautiful valley of the Torridge – a land in which to lose yourself; a land of woods, streams and sleepy hamlets. To the south of Roborough is Dolton and the nearby beauty spot of Halsdon, which is now a nature reserve. It was here that one of the great love stories of World War II played out, between the well-known poet and glass engraver Laurence Whistler and the poet and actress Jill Furse.

Laurence Whistler grew up in Salisbury, in the shadow of his flamboyant elder brother, Rex, who was also an artist. Unlike his brother, however, Laurence was shy and retiring, and it was through his sheer dedication to glass engraving – along with his brother's encouragement – that he revived the craft throughout England.

In 1939, Laurence married Jill Furse in a quiet ceremony at Salisbury Cathedral and, soon after, the couple settled in a remote cottage here in the Torridge valley. Although the war cast a deep shadow over the Whistler family, with both brothers called up for active service, Jill and Laurence lived an idyllic life when Laurence was on leave. In his moving memoir, *The Initials in the Heart: A Celebration of Love*, Whistler said that he and his wife had little and wanted little: 'Simplicity of living, happiness, beauty of season and place, came together in extraordinary contrast with the anguish of the western world.' Sadly, Jill became ill and died shortly after the birth of their second child, in 1944. The artist described their marriage as 'both ideally happy, yet cruelly short'. It is one of the most moving love stories of the war years. Jill's death was followed, in 1950, by Laurence's unsuccessful union with her younger sister, Theresa. The couple had two children together, but the marriage was later dissolved.

Another tragedy befell Laurence in 1944, when his brother, Rex, died in service in Normandy. He is remembered by Laurence's extraordinary revolving glass sculpture, which can be seen today in Salisbury Cathedral. The triangular prism shows, successively, the scenes most familiar to the Whistler boys: the spire and chapter house in Salisbury, the family home of Walton Canonry and the birds wheeling around the soaring cathedral spire. Laurence's other work can be seen in various places in the West Country, but most spectacularly at Moreton church near Dorchester. Here, he engraved all 13 windows in the church after it was bombed by the Germans in 1940.

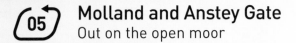

05 Molland and Anstey Gate
Out on the open moor

409m

334m

M

8km

3.5hrs

-2.5km

Somerset

Devon

Dorset

Cornwall

This walk, which weaves its way through a web of interlinking footpaths, many of which don't feature on even the most detailed maps, is a great introduction to Exmoor. Taking in farms, woods and expansive open moorland, the route includes some extended climbs that are more than made up for by the incredible views from Anstey Gate – the boundary between West Anstey Common and Molland Moor, which is marked by a hedge and cattle grid. Remember to take a compass with you – this will be invaluable when it comes to helping you distinguish one path from another, as well as sighting more distant goals. Do not, under any circumstances, undertake this walk in foggy conditions: not only would that be extremely dangerous, but you'd also miss the magnificent views of the North Devon countryside that define the route.

05 Molland and Anstey Gate
Out on the open moor

White Post

Clogg's Down

Cloggs Farm

Moorhouse Ridge

Long Breach

Black Ball

Round Hill

N

400m
1,000ft

Molland Common

White Moor

Anstey Gate

5 ★

Luckworthy

6

300

4

Smallacombe

3

Brimblecombe

7

Ringcombe

MOLLAND

2

Gourte Farm

Ringcombe

1 ★

10

9

8

Pond

Combe

Stone

Bremley

200

200

Deer's Leap Farm

5km

Pulworthy

200

Beer Farm

Slade

CLIMBS

400m
375m
350m
325m
300m
275m
250m

1km 2km 3km 4km 5km 6km 7km 8km

Hall Farm

GETTING THERE

Molland is a small village located just to the south of Exmoor National Park. You can find it by driving roughly east on the A361 out of South Molton. Turn left onto the B3227 and follow signs for Molland for about 3 miles. Park near the church when you reach the village and locate our first Pitstop, the London Inn (see p.57). EX36 3NG.

WALK DIRECTIONS

1 Once parked up near the church, follow the road past the London Inn and turn right at a junction leading uphill. Walk past a farm (on your left) and join the farm track briefly, before forking off to the right across the first field and continuing on the same bearing across the second.

NOT TO MISS

St Mary's church

This medieval church, which was built on the site of a much earlier church and then remodelled in the 16th and 17th centuries, retains many historic features, having escaped the hands of Victorian restorers. These include a Norman font from the original church, a magnificent three-decker pulpit and box pews – both of which date from the 18th century – and, in the doorway, the village stocks, a reminder of brutal times past. It's said that, in the 19th century, the clerk here had a stave with a wooden ball at one end and feathers at the other. Any man who fell asleep during a service was hit on the head with the ball; any lady guilty of the same folly was tickled with the feathers. A stone 'heart box' contains the hearts of the local Courtenay family, rather than those of crusaders – of whom only the heart was returned for entombment – as is usually the case.

2 On the far side of the second field, go through the gate and cross the lane to join the path almost directly opposite. Walk along the right-hand edge of this field and then, when the field edge turns away to the right, walk diagonally left downhill to a footbridge. (If you reach a footbridge without a gate, walk past it with the stream on your right to the next footbridge.) Go over the stream here, through the gate and diagonally left uphill to another gate, located halfway up the hill. Now follow the path along to the field corner, where there's a lane.

3 Turn left onto the lane, then almost immediately right down the narrow lane next to the Smallacombe sign. Walk along and past the house to the valley bottom. Ignore the bridleway sign; instead, stay on the track and go through the gate, over the small bridge and onto the moorland.

4 Follow the main track as it leads you uphill in a northeasterly direction. After about 100m, you reach a junction. Take the smaller path straight ahead by forking left. (If you fork right here, you will be on the shortcut route – see below.) At first, you will have a shallow valley on your left. The path continues up onto open moorland where it might be indistinct. Keep going roughly northeast and incredible views will open up around you. At a point after about 1km, you will walk past a sparse collection of small trees and the path bends slightly to the right. You will now be following a bearing of ENE towards the top of the hill. After 200m, at a fork, go left. As you near the top, the path becomes narrower and then widens out again. Keep going as your bearing turns more to the right (east) – roughly in the direction of a solitary, medium-sized tree – and you will arrive at a junction with an asphalt lane where there's a gate and a cattle grid. If you meet the lane at a different point, you're likely to be west of the cattle grid. Simply walk to the right along the lane.

SHORTCUT – By forking right at the junction mentioned at the beginning of Instruction 4, you'll shorten the route by about an hour, or roughly 2.5km. Once on the wider path, follow for a few metres and then let it lead you to the left, along a field boundary, which will be on your right. This bridleway will lead you for about 1.5km, for the most part alongside the field boundary. You should have moorland uphill to your left and farmers' fields downhill to the right pretty much all the way. After just over 1km, you will walk through a wooded area; keep going through to the other side. About 250m after you exit the other side of the woods, there will be a T-junction. Turn right to walk downhill. You are now on the well-made track to Bremley mentioned in Instruction 6.

5 Go over the cattle grid and turn right sharply off the lane, onto a path heading downhill (south), which follows a hedgerow on your right. There is also a smallish farm building on the right just as you enter the field. Be sure to admire the views before you descend – from here, you can see the hills of Devon's other national park, Dartmoor.

6 When you reach a T-junction of paths, turn right and go through a gate. After about 250m, follow the main path to the left and downhill on a well-made track signposted Bremley. (This is where the shortcut rejoins the route.) Follow the track out of the moorland area. Go through a gate and continue downhill on a concrete track.

NOT TO MISS

Anstey Gate
To the east and north, rural Somerset and wild Exmoor stretch out before you; to the south and west is the magnificent Devon countryside.

7 You will soon reach a house. Look for the path that runs between hedgerows in a kind of tunnel to the right; there will be a blue arrow to help you find it. It runs along below the garage. After about 200m, once you are in the wooded area, continue straight ahead (right) at the junction and keep going till you meet a footbridge. Cross the bridge, turn right, walk 50m alongside the stream and then fork left and uphill into the woods. Ignoring turn-offs, follow the main path through the woods for 400m, until you arrive at some fields where you should join a track. This will lead you along the field edge and downhill to a farm. Join the lane here to continue downhill.

8 Walking downhill on the lane, go past the pond, over the cattle grid and then around the bend to a junction. Turn right here (which effectively means you walk straight ahead) at the junction and follow the steep lane downhill into the valley, where there is a small bridge.

9 Just after the bridge, turn right onto the pathway and up the steps. In the field, follow the path up the short, steep section and ahead to the stile. (You will see several gates leading out of this field, but only one stile.) Go over the stile and follow the right-hand field border in the next three fields, and you'll come out at a lane junction.

10 Walk straight ahead onto the lane signposted Molland. Follow this sleepy lane for the final 750m or so to the village and the church where you started.

THE PITSTOPS

The London Inn
This traditional pub, deep in the heart of Exmoor, serves hearty, home-cooked family meals. The atmosphere is relaxed, the service is excellent and the Sunday roasts are legendary.
Molland, South Molton EX36 3NG
Open Mon 6–11, Tue–Sat 12.30–2.30 & 6–11, Sun midday–4 & 7–11
01769 550269. www.londoninnmolland.co.uk

The Blackcock Inn
Walkers flock to this friendly pub, with its good grub, fine ales and lovely garden. There's also a campsite and swimming pool here.
Molland, South Molton EX36 3NW
Open Mon–Thu midday–midnight, Fri & Sat midday–2, Sun midday–midnight
01769 550297. www.theblackcockinn.org

THE EXTRA STEP

Stargazing on Exmoor, past and present

Almost entirely empty, stunningly silent and pitch dark at night, Exmoor offers some of the best stargazing in the country. One of only a handful of designated International Dark Sky Reserves in the world, the moor was the first site in Europe to make the grade, back in 2011. The area has an extremely low level of artificial light pollution, offering great opportunities, on clear nights, to take in the glittering firmament. The darkness here is so absolute that you can see around 3,000 stars with the naked eye alone – a far cry from the 200 or so you might be lucky enough to spot in London on the clearest of nights. The sad truth is that throughout much of England, creeping urbanisation and the ubiquitous use of streetlights have made such magnificent visions a rarity in the 21st century.

The moor extends across two counties, Somerset and Devon, with much of the management of the moor in the hands of Exmoor National Park, which works closely with local landowners, including the National Trust. There are visitor centres at Dunster and Lynmouth, but the closest to Molland is actually in the pretty village of Dulverton in West Somerset. Here, as well as acquiring information about the moor, with its complex ecology and fantastic array of flora and fauna, you can hire a telescope and head out to see the Milky Way, with its meteors, planets and constellations, in mind-boggling detail. Some of the best spots from which to gaze upwards on Exmoor include Landacre Bridge – to the north of Molland – Brendon Two Gates, Dunkery Beacon (the highest point on Exmoor) and Webber's Post – in the middle of the moor – and Haddon Hill and Wimbleball Lake, to the east of Dulverton. Having said that, pretty well anywhere you go that has an unbroken view of the sky will offer superb viewing on a clear night. Much of the moor is open access, so it's up to you whether you roam freely or stick to the extensive network of footpaths.

To complete the experience, a daylight detour to the remains of the Bronze Age Porlock Stone Circle, on the park's northern boundary, might well be in order. This ancient monument is thought to have been built according to some sort of celestial alignment – a poignant reminder that mankind's fascination with the sparkling skies of night are as old as time itself.

319m

390m

M

10.5km

3hrs

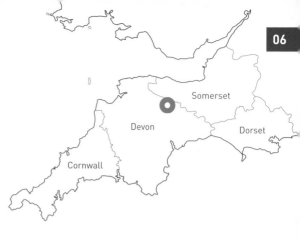

Somerset

Devon

Dorset

Cornwall

An extended stroll through farmland, woodland and open fields on the edge of Exmoor National Park, this route is generally easy-going, though you'll encounter a handful of significant climbs. The hedgerows that line the way are rich in wild food at certain times of year, so keep your eyes peeled for berries and nuts as you go; a wild-food guide might be handy, as there's a much richer harvest than just blackberries to be picked here. There's also an abundance of wildlife in these parts, so keep alert and cameras at the ready. Remember to shut the gates to fields. If you time your walk well, you'll receive a warm welcome and a great pint in each of the local pubs.

East Loosemoor

High Bolham

Oakfordbridge

Wonham Hou

Bowdens

N

300m
1,000ft

Hamslade House

OAKFORD

Stuckeridge House

5

Manor House

4

3

6

7

Iron Mill Stream

2

8

9

Hangman's Hill Cross

Wheatland

Great Coleford

12

Quoit-at-Cross

Ash

11

13

1

10

14

STOODLEIGH

Kissing Gate Cross

Castle

Rull

Vial's Corner

Ford Barton

Webland

West End Cross

Rifton

CLIMBS

300m
275m
250m
225m
200m
175m

1km 2km 3km 4km 5km 6km 7km 8km 9km 10km

Rifton Moor

GETTING THERE

Stoodleigh is located to the northwest of Tiverton, about halfway between the A361 and the A396. Wide areas or lay-bys are dotted along the road that runs through the village. Park as near to our first Pitstop, the Stoodleigh Inn (see p.67), as you can – the road just near it is quite wide. EX16 9PR.

WALK DIRECTIONS

1 Walk to the Stoodleigh Inn from where you parked on the road that runs through the village. With the pub on your right, walk ahead, slightly downhill and away from the village. After about 750m, on a sweeping right-hand bend, turn left onto the pathway. Bear slightly right in the field towards the gate and then follow the right-hand field border in the next two fields to a track. Walk ahead on the track for 200m until you reach the lane.

2 Turn left onto the lane and follow it for about 450m to the junction. Turn right, signposted Oakford, and follow this small lane downhill for about 1km into a wooded valley. You will go around some sharp bends and then meet a bridge over a stream.

3 Go over the bridge and then, after a few metres, turn left to walk along a concrete track with the stream on your left. Walk past a row of terraced cottages, ignore the steep track to the right just after, but keep going to a small parking area. At the time of writing, there was a house being constructed near the parking area, but the public right of way you are on should lead you slightly right and uphill on a wide pathway through the woods. Let it lead you left and up the side of the valley. After about 250m, fork right onto a steeper path where you see the yellow arrow – keep going uphill for about another 200m to the stile.

NOT TO MISS

St Peter's church
Although there's been a church on this site in Oakford since the 13th century, the battlemented tower you see today dates from the 15th century and the rest of the building from the 1830s, when it underwent restoration work after a fire. The large, light interior is known for its embroidered and colourful kneelers, which beautifully complement the richness of the stained-glass windows.

4 Go over the stile and follow the left-hand field edge to join a track leading off from the first corner and follow along to the farm. Fork right when you are within the farm-building area itself, and walk ahead to the lane. You are now in Oakford and just under halfway along the route.

OPTIONAL EXTRA – Now's your chance to stop for refreshment at our second Pitstop, the Red Lion Hotel (see p.67). Simply turn right onto the lane and walk for a short distance – you'll find it easily enough.

5 Turn left onto the lane to continue the route. Walk uphill for about 200m and then turn left onto the footpath. Walk diagonally right across the large field to the midpoint on the far side, where you will find a gate. Go through this to the next field and turn right to follow the right-hand edge of two fields to the bottom right-hand corner, where you should join a track to the right. Walk 50m or so until you reach the lane.

6 Cross over the lane and go up the steps onto the footpath. Go through two gates then walk diagonally left across the field – there will be a house away to your left. Go through a gap in the hedge to another field. Ignore the gate diagonally to the left; instead, go straight ahead to the bottom left-hand corner of the field to reach a gate under the trees.

NOT TO MISS
Wild food
In the late summer and early autumn, you'll find the trees and plants along this section bursting with nuts and berries. Look out for hazelnuts, elderberries, wild strawberries and raspberries, blackberries, bilberries, beechnuts and sloes. Remember to carry a basket or bag with you.

7 Pass through the gate, walk across the field to the bottom corner and go through the gate on the left. Follow the right-hand field edge to another gate. Go through and walk directly downhill into a valley. You will see a lane ahead that rises up the other side to the right. Head towards the lane and go over the stream. Follow the lane 50m or so to the building and then the lane.

8 Turn right onto the lane and follow for 150m or so. Just over the brow of the hill, turn left onto a track that cuts back on you. (There is a gate next to it on the right.)

9 Follow this track and, after 200m, fork left, downhill at the junction. After a further 1km along this pretty section, you arrive at a lane.

10 Turn left onto the lane then, after 50m or so, turn left again onto the signposted public bridleway – be sure to fork right and walk alongside the stream.

11 Follow this track for about 600m, going through three gates and then uphill in a field that makes a perfect picnic spot. After this field, continue the route by following right-hand field edges. Go downhill, over a stream and then uphill to meet a track. Turn right onto the track and walk about 300m to the lane. Turn right onto the lane and walk 150m to the crossroads.

12 At the crossroads, turn right, signposted Stoodleigh. After about 500m on the lane, you will see a 'V' entrance to a track. Look ahead and you will see a footpath sign and stile – this is a pathway that effectively forks off to the left from the lane. Join this and follow the left-hand field edge. Go over a stile in the field corner and then walk to your right. Go through a gate and you will emerge at a lane junction.

13 At the lane, walk past the bench onto the lane signposted Stoodleigh and Tiverton. After about 100m, turn right onto the pathway just after the entrance to Stoodleigh Court. Follow this wide path for about 500m to the lane. Be sure to enjoy this section – the old path to the church (see below).

14 At the lane, with the church directly ahead of you, turn left and walk the final 150m to the T-junction where the Stoodleigh Inn and start point of the walk is a few metres along to your right.

NOT TO MISS
St Margaret's church
A 15th-century church restored in the 19th century, St Margaret's (see also p.69) in Stoodleigh has a peal of six bells, which have recently been rehung. With advanced notice, visiting bell-ringers are welcome.

THE PITSTOPS

The Stoodleigh Inn

This small village local, which has an open fire and real ales, is known for its quiz nights and skittles. Bar snacks are under £5. Stoodleigh, Tiverton EX16 9PR. Open Thu–Sat 7–11 & Sun midday–2 & 7–11. 01398 351357

The Red Lion Hotel

This welcoming inn, which has been recently refurbished, serves delicious homemade dishes using local produce wherever possible. Rookery Hill, Oakford EX16 9ES. Open Mon 6–10, Tue–Thu midday–3 & 6–10, Fri & Sat midday–3 & 5.30–11 & Sun midday–8 01398 351592. www.redlionoakford.co.uk

THE EXTRA STEP

Stoodleigh's ancient roots

Stoodleigh weighs heavy with history, from its ancient sites and Norman church font to grisly-sounding Hangman's Hill. It's a place where tales and folklore abound, and where the past seems ever-present. And what better spot to kick off a historical tour of a community than at its church, which, in Stoodleigh's case, is 15th-century St Margaret's. Although the church underwent extensive renovations in the 19th century, the tower is thought to have been built when the yew tree in the churchyard was planted, some 500 years ago. The handsome stone structure is surrounded by cottages and four footpaths that enter the churchyard, one of which leads to the 'big house', Stoodleigh Court, built in 1881.

However, the building's rather plain façade gives little notion of the glories within. These include the Norman church font, which formed part of an earlier parish church, and one of the most impressive collections of painted wooden roof bosses in the West Country, which are as close to folk art as English church decoration comes. Their purpose was to convey the word of God, including the seven deadly sins, to illiterate peasants who could not understand the Latin Mass. Wall plates, which sit where the roof and walls meet, depict green men and foliage – these are deeply pagan in origin, having been incorporated into the symbolism of the late medieval church. Roman tiles have also been discovered here.

The inhabitants of this historic village, which is mentioned in the Domesday Book, tell a great many tales about its history, including that of Gibbet Moor, the site of the gibbet where sheep-stealers got their comeuppance. Locals have been known to recount how their great-great grandparents watched the last man hanged up on the moor. And then there's Hangman's Hill, another ominous-sounding local landmark, that's said to have got its name after an old sea dog returned home from sea to be greeted by a crone with her pet crow perched on her shoulder. The poor fellow was so frightened, so the story goes, that he took a rope and hanged himself.

But that's not all in the way of local fable. Legend has it that nearby Stoodleigh Beacon was one of the warning beacons during the Spanish Armada. Going back even further than that, the village has two ancient sites: Quoit-at-Cross (SS917190), an old burial ground, and Castle Close (SS937181), an Iron Age enclosure.

187m

289m

H

10km

4hrs

+1.5km

#1 -1.5km
#2 -5km

Somerset

Devon

Dorset

Cornwall

Encompassing a stroll through the woods, a meander along the river, a ramble along a hill ridge boasting magnificent countryside views and a couple of challenging hill climbs, this walk has something for everyone. As you walk, keep an eye out for fruits and berries on the hedgerows, which offer some welcome fuel for your journey. But if wild food isn't enough to keep you going, take the short detour to Bickleigh, a beautiful, historic village with two pubs. Here, on a hot summer's day, a cooling paddle is almost always in order at the riverside Fisherman's Cot pub – the one-time haunt of folk-rock duo Simon and Garfunkel in the 1960s. It's wise to wear wellies on this walk, which can get wet and very muddy in places.

CLIMBS

GETTING THERE

Cadeleigh is a village located to the southwest of Tiverton, just off the A3072 near Bickleigh. When you arrive in the village, park in the car park of our first Pitstop, the Cadeleigh Arms (see p.75). Be sure to ask permission from the landlord, with the promise of your business later on. EX16 8HP.

WALK DIRECTIONS

1 After parking, join the road by turning right and walk past the front entrance of the Cadeleigh Arms, which will be on your right. At the first junction, turn right, signposted to the Parish Hall & Little Silver. Turn left at the village hall car park to walk along the public footpath, uphill slightly on the driveway, towards the house. Or, if you are taking our first shortcut, then keep going towards Little Silver and pick up the instructions below. Following the main route, it may feel like you are straying onto private property, but you can rest assured that this is a public right of way. Go past the house, through the gate and into the field.

SHORTCUT #1 – This is the second half of the walk, included because it is less hilly than the first half. It cuts only 1.5km from the route but it follows a pretty bridleway next to the River Dart. In Instruction 1, where indicated, keep going along the narrow, sleepy lane, steep in parts, to Little Silver. As you arrive, you will see a collection of houses. Walk around a bend and go past a bridleway and thatched cottage. Keep walking along the road as it turns uphill and pick up from Instruction 6 below.

2 Follow the left-hand edge of the field, go through the gate on the right and follow the left-hand edge in the next two fields. In the fourth field, follow the left-hand edge again, but halfway down the hill, head to the right and down to the lane. Turn left on the lane and then go over a stile on the left after a few metres. Go through the next gate, then ahead (left) onto the track. After 50m, bear right to go through another gate and follow the right-hand field edge. Go through to the next field, walk ahead to the stile and then go over the stream.

3 After the stream, walk uphill along the right-hand edge of the field, over the stile and into the woods. Follow the markings through the woods and be sure not to miss the arrow and path downhill through the gap in the trees. Coming out of the woods, turn left and follow the path along the bottom of the woods and then over a small stream.

4 You'll find yourself in another field. Walk diagonally left, uphill, and go through the gap in the hedgerow to the next field. Follow the left-hand edge and then follow ahead into the next field and walk diagonally left for about 100m to the small lane. Turn right onto the lane and walk down to the farm buildings.

5 After the first few buildings, you should see the cattle pen on the left. Just here, fork left and go through to the adjoining field on the left – there should be a footpath sign, but it may be overgrown. Follow the right-hand field edges for the next few hundred metres, mostly downhill, until you reach a wide bridleway or track on the right that leads downhill. Follow this to a lane. This is Little Silver and the point at which our first shortcut ends (see p.73) and our second begins (see below).

SHORTCUT #2 – If the first half of the walk, with its superb views, are enough for you, then you can cut the walk short from Little Silver by turning right on the lane in Instruction 5. Keep going on the tiny lane, which has a very steep uphill section, back past Cadeleigh village hall and then turn left at the T-junction to the start. This shortcut is the first shortcut in reverse.

6 Reaching the lane, you will have a small thatched cottage on your left. Turn left onto the lane and walk past the other houses and uphill. After about 150m, turn right (almost back on yourself) onto a public bridleway. This will lead you, for about 2km, to a lane near Bickleigh. It's easy to follow, especially if you look out for the following landmarks: after about 300m, you enter some woods; after about 750m, you walk past three large ponds on the left; and after 1.2km, you will briefly have the River Dart on your left. Don't go over the footbridge or ford here – keep going on the bridleway for a further 800m to the lane.

OPTIONAL EXTRA – If you want to visit Bickleigh and our second Pitstop, the Fisherman's Cot (see opposite), turn left onto the lane and then left again at the junction. This will add just under 1.5km to the walk length.

7 To continue the route, turn right onto the lane and walk uphill. After 100m, fork left onto a smaller lane, almost a track, and start following footpath signs. Go past the houses and, after the first farm building, fork right. At the next fork, go left, past more farm buildings, and the lane will turn into a dirt track. Keep following the track for a good 500m, until you arrive at a gate and a field. Go straight ahead in the field to the gate halfway up the boundary opposite. Go through this and follow the footpath signs past Cadeleigh Court – left at the first T-junction, right at the second and then all the way for about 1km on a concrete farm track to a lane.

8 Turn right, uphill on the lane and, after 250m, turn left onto the footpath between hedgerows. Follow this uphill, sticking to the main path and going through gates when required, to the lane at the top.

9 Turn right, then right again onto a final sleepy lane that will lead you for 500m all the way back to Cadeleigh, a welcoming pub and the start point.

THE PITSTOPS

The Cadeleigh Arms

A newly renovated, community-owned pub, the Cadeleigh Arms manages to retain much of the atmosphere of its popular previous incarnation. It's a bustling place serving an array of pub favourites, from fish and chips to Thai curries, at very reasonable prices. Cadeleigh, Tiverton EX16 8HP. Open Mon 6–11, Tue–Sat noon–2.30 & 6–11, Sun noon–3. 01884 855238. www.cadeleigh.com

The Fisherman's Cot

This picturesque pub, perched right on the banks of the River Exe, is a popular all-round choice. The relaxing and homely interior provides the perfect backdrop to a warming winter's meal, while the outside seating area, beside the racing river, is lovely in summer. Expect mid-priced comfort food, from burgers to pies. Bickleigh, Tiverton EX16 8RW. Open Mon–Sat 11–11, Sun 11–10.30 01884 855237. www.fishermanscotpub.co.uk

THE EXTRA STEP

The River Exe, from Tiverton to Exeter

Devon's main river – the name of which comes from the Celtic word Isca, or water – virtually bisects the county, beginning its journey at Exe Head on Exmoor and flowing south for 80km through some of the county's most beautiful countryside, before emptying out into the English Channel. For much of its course, the meandering Exe and its tributaries flow through pastoral landscapes, narrow, steep-sided valleys and open moorland. At high tide, the river swells and the estuary becomes a popular place for watersports; at low tide, the mudflats are exposed to become an important feeding source for wading birds, particularly wintering waders.

The Exe Valley Way is a long-distance path that runs the length of the river, passing through the town of Tiverton, where the power of the water was used in the 16th and 17th centuries for the booming wool industry, and the cathedral city of Exeter, once an important trading port, on its route from source to sea. Between these two communities, the Exe Valley combines stretches of wild Devon with more suburban areas. Along this 25km stretch lies the small village of Bickleigh, with its pretty grey-stone bridge of five arches, which was built in the Middle Ages and enlarged in 1809. According to the locals, this structure inspired Simon and Garfunkel's 1970 hit, *Bridge over Troubled Water* – the musical duo are said to have visited Bickleigh and the Fisherman's Cot (see p.75), a pub on the west side of the river, in 1969.

Much more picturesque and historic than the Fisherman's Cot, however, is the nearby Trout Inn, a traditional thatched building with roses climbing up the walls. In one of the pub's fireplaces is a stone inscribed with the date 1722, which was taken from the bridge during an early repair job. Opposite is the Grade II-listed Bickleigh Cottage Guest House, a thatched 17th-century building. Even older is historic Bickleigh Castle, which has a Norman chapel that's thought to be the oldest existing building in Devon. Its modern-day role as a wedding and conference venue is a far cry from its glory days during the English Civil War.

The village's old railway station explores more recent local history, in the form of its model railway centre. Though it's strictly in Bickleigh, this station on the Exeter to Dulverton line was called Cadeleigh to avoid confusion with the other Bickleigh, near Plymouth. Sadly, the line was closed in 1965 when the network was reduced, putting an end to Devon's rural branch lines. For a dose of modernity in an otherwise historic place, Bickleigh Mill is a vast shopping, dining and entertainment complex situated on the east bank of the river and set within a working mill.

Roadford Lake
The birds and the bees

 267m

 235m

 E

 7.5km

 2.5hrs

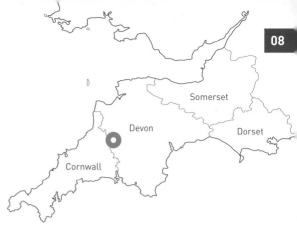

Somerset

Devon

Dorset

Cornwall

This walk, which winds its way through pasture and woodland, offers beautiful views and jaw-dropping biodiversity, from trees and plants to birds, insects and livestock. You'll start and finish beside Roadford Lake, a man-made reservoir dating from 1989 that holds more than 34.5 billion litres of water, making it the largest area of fresh water in the Southwest. The lake's northernmost third is a designated special-protection area, providing overwintering birds and other wildlife with a safe habitat. The majority of the rest of the lake is used for fishing, sailing and other watersports. With no particularly steep climbs, this walk can be undertaken by almost anyone. You'll want to keep the pace slow, in order to take in as much of the area's natural riches as possible. Remember to take extra care not to disturb any wildlife habitat you come across.

Witherdon

Boldventure

Eworthy

Bovey

200

200

200

150

Parsonage
Cross

150

GERMANSWEEK

150

7

Southweek
Wood

6

5

Redstone

200

150

8

9 Southweek

150

150

Bird Hide

1

2

150

Toft

3

4

150

150

Breazle
Farms

150

★ 3km

N

400m
1,000ft

CLIMBS

275m
250m
225m
200m
175m

1km 2km 3km 4km 5km 6km 7km 8km

Roadford

Headson Cross

Headson

GETTING THERE

Roadford Lake is a large reservoir just north of the A30 between Launceston and Okehampton. We haven't given a postcode for sat-nav devices as the closest will take you quite far from the start point. To get there, turn off the A30 when you see the signs for Broadwoodwidger. Drive up the eastern side of Roadford Lake towards Bratton Clovelly and then Germansweek. This will lead you to the road bridge in the northeast corner of the lake. Just before the bridge, park in the large parking bay on the left-hand side of the road.

WALK DIRECTIONS

1 Walk away from the bridge a short distance and you will see three gates on your right. The right-hand gate leads to the bird hide featured in our Not To Miss below. To start the walk, go through the left-hand gate and along the public bridleway within the woods.

NOT TO MISS
Bird hide
This hide offers superb views across the lake, which is one of the most important inland sites for wildfowl in Devon. Its interior walls are covered with pictures of the vast array of species in the area, from Canada geese to mallards to great-crested grebes. Whether or not you're a serious twitcher, this hide will open your eyes to the staggering variety of wildlife supported by the lake. (SX435929)

2 The bridleway roughly follows the edge of the lake. You will get some pretty glimpses of water through the trees on your right and peaceful farmland on your left. Stay on this path until your reach a sign that directs you left onto a bridleway between hedgerows. Walk up this bridleway, away from the lake, and you'll encounter some magnificent views across the lake. After about 500m, you arrive at a road.

3 Cross over the road and join the bridleway opposite. Keep going on this track for a further 500m, until you arrive in a field where the track disappears. Walk directly ahead across the field, aiming for the far right-hand corner. Do not walk downhill at all.

4 Go through the gate in the corner and follow the bridleway along the left-hand field edge. This continues along several fields for about 1.5km, until you arrive at a track. Go ahead, ignore the driveway on the left after a few metres and continue 200m to the lane.

5 Turn left onto the lane and walk 200m, then turn right onto the pathway through the field. Walk ahead and downhill in the field, with the gate directly behind you. When the bottom field edge comes into view, walk diagonally to your left and locate a stile under the trees.

6 Go over the stile and after a pretty but steep downhill section in the woods, you arrive at a junction. Turn left to go through a gate and then fork left after a few metres. After about 150m, go through a gate and follow the right-hand field edge. In the next field, walk to the far right-hand corner and go over the stile into the woods.

THE PITSTOP

Lakeside

With its superb lakeside views, appealing menu, children's play area and gift shop, this café is well loved by people of all ages – especially walkers and watersports enthusiasts in need of a calorie hit after their exertions in and around the lake. Expect light lunches, homemade cakes and ice creams, including plenty of gluten-free options. As far as possible, ingredients are locally sourced.
Roadford Lake, Broadwoodwidger, Lifton PL16 0RL
Open daily 10–4. 01566 784859. www.lakesideroadford.org.uk

7 After a short section on the woodland pathway, go over a stile to join a track. Follow this for about 750m – you will have the sound of a stream to your right and birdsong all around. Be sure to keep an eye out for the bird-watching tower on your left.

8 At the end of the track you arrive at a field. Go through the gate and along the left-hand field border, where you will be rewarded with commanding views over the lake.

9 About 100m after passing the house, you will see a gate on the left. Go through the gate and turn left. Walk 100m to the junction, where you will see the parking bay where you started the walk.

THE EXTRA STEP

Lydford's tumultuous past

The village of Lydford, which lies roughly 12km southeast of Roadford Lake, is a great place to contemplate the rise and fall of the county's rich history. Established in the late 9th century by Alfred the Great, King of Wessex, for its strategic military position, Lydford (known then as Hlidaford or Hlidan) was an important Anglo-Saxon town – it was a bulwark against Celtic Cornwall to the west and violent rampages from Danish Vikings to the east. In these early years, the town minted its own coins, Lydford Silver Pennies, which were made using local silver; many of these coins ended up in Scandinavia after the Danes ransacked Lydford in 927.

By the Middle Ages, Lydford was a wealthy coinage town and, thanks to its position in the heart of tin-mining country, its castle became a grim prison and court of law where those who broke local stannary law were tried and incarcerated. Punishments metered out to inmates could be severe; the penalty for fraudulently adulterating tin, for example, was three spoonfuls of the molten variety poured down the offender's throat. Inmates included Richard Strode, a Member of Parliament whose crime was to speak out about the need to reform stannary laws. As a consequence of the harsh conduct he received in prison, parliament put in place what we now recognise as parliamentary immunity – the freedom of MPs to speak their minds. The castle is now under the protection of English Heritage; watch out for the deep drops and precarious staircases within its walls.

Running alongside the castle is the beautiful Lydford Gorge, the deepest gorge in the Southwest. This beauty spot is home to the formidable Devil's Cauldron, a series of whirlpools in the River Lyd, and the graceful White Lady Waterfall, a thin, twisting line of white water that plunges 30m into the gorge. It's said that the flow of the falls was once controlled by a miller, who, in exchange for sixpence from visitors, would open the sluice gates of his millpond to enhance the effect of its tumbling water.

The gorge wasn't always so appealing. In the 17th century, it was a dangerous place to be, roamed by the notorious Gubbins family, a network of sheep-stealing scoundrels who terrorised local farmers. By the 19th century, however, with foreign travel discouraged during the Napoleonic Wars, tourists visited Lydford on the newly built railways, flocking to this verdant wilderness area, with its wildlife, whirlpools and waterfall, in their droves. Now owned by the National Trust, the gorge is as majestic today as it was then. If you can get beyond the treacherous Devil's Cauldron, you'll be amply rewarded by Ticker's Pool, where light filters down through the leaves of towering beech trees as grey wagtails go about their business at the water's edge.

 403m

 291m

 E

 6.5km

 2hrs

 -0.5km

Somerset

Dorset

Devon

Cornwall

This walk is a great introduction to Dartmoor, offering fabulous countryside views and a gentle meander along the East Okement River – and all without having to worry about getting lost among the tors. Having said that, it's advisable to carry a map and compass with you at all times in these parts, just in case you get into difficulty. Sturdy walking boots are also essential, as some of the paths next to the river are rocky and can get slippery after rainfall. Otherwise, expect idyllic woodland, rushing water, stepping stones, waterfalls, picnic spots and some of the region's best wild swimming.

OKEHAMPTON

Ball Hill

Westlake

Station Road

Parklands

Tors Road

Camp Road

East Hill

Well Cross

Lower Halstock

Moorgate Fm

Higher Halstock

Cullever

Museum

Exeter Road

Crediton Road

B3260

Fatherford Lane

Fatherford Lane

A30

Moor Brook

East Okement River

Old Rectory Farm

Wild Swimm

N

200m
500ft

CLIMBS

400m
350m
300m
250m
200m

0.5km 1.0km 1.5km 2.0km 2.5km 3.0km 3.5km 4.0km 4.5km 5.0km 5.5km 6.0km

GETTING THERE

Find your way to the railway station. As you approach from the direction of the town, go under the bridge and then left into the rear car park. EX20 1EH.

WALK DIRECTIONS

1 Near the car park, follow the sign marked 'Pedestrian Route to Dartmoor' – go left and uphill on the lane. After 100m, turn left onto the pathway. After a further 50m, fork right and then, after 100m, turn right onto a path that leads you over the A30 on a footbridge.

2 On the other side of the footbridge, turn right and, almost immediately, fork left onto a smaller path. Follow this uphill to a wider path and turn right to walk uphill to a gate in the far left-hand (top) corner of the field.

3 Go through the gate and straight ahead onto the lane. After 100m, turn left onto the path that runs alongside the field border to another lane. Here, turn left, joining the lane briefly to go over the cattle grid, fork off the lane to the left and walk uphill on the wide grassy pathway. This takes you to the top of East Hill.

4 From the top of East Hill, you have some magnificent views of two of Dartmoor's most northerly tors on your right and North Devon's hills and dales on your left. From the top, turn right and walk between gorse bushes downhill to rejoin the lane. Walk downhill on the lane and turn left onto the pathway after 150m (before the bridge). Walk across the field and go over the stile into the woodland. The path follows the course of a small river called Moor Brook. After 200m along this pretty section, turn right to pass over the stepping stones and uphill on a pathway.

SHORTCUT – Instead of going over the stepping stones, keep going along this path next to Moor Brook. After about 500m, you will arrive at another river – the East Okemont. Turn left and you will be back on the main route at Instruction 7. This shortcut cuts about 500m off the route and avoids a hill.

5 After a few metres of walking uphill on the pathway, turn left at the junction and follow the path that roughly runs along the upper edge of the woodland. You will pass through a couple of fields and arrive at a point where you start to descend into the woods again. After a few metres, make sure you fork left onto a smaller pathway that runs more steeply downhill – it's just next to a distinctive-looking tree that has grown with three trunks. This will take you all the way down to the valley bottom and the East Okemont River.

6 Arriving at the East Okemont, turn left where you see a small wooden post and follow the pathway. After a rocky first section, the route quickly evens out and you can enjoy the numerous bathing and picnic spots along the way.

NOT TO MISS

Wild swimming

Look for the numerous deep pools in the river, which are ideal spots for wild swimming. Please take utmost care after heavy rain, as the current can quickly sweep you down river and into danger.

7 After 400m or so, you will arrive at an old wall. Walk to the right around this and then over the footbridge. This is where the shortcut rejoins the route. Keep going along the East Okemont River after the footbridge and, after a further 500m, you will pass under the A30 and arrive at a bridge. Cross over this, then turn left. After a few metres, go through the gate, past the house and after the parking area, left onto a path.

8 This wide path takes you into the conservation area known as Ball Hill. You will walk alongside a stream and a path with ancient stone walls that hint at the age of this pretty route.

9 On the far side of the conservation area, you arrive at a junction. Fork left onto the path that continues alongside the stream. Walk over the footbridge into the playing fields and stay on the path to walk along the river again. You will walk past another footbridge – do not go over this one, but keep going until you see the next one, after about 300m.

10 Go over the footbridge and up the hill on the steps. Keep to the main path and you will arrive at a lane at the top – turn left and you will recognise Okehampton Station. Go under the bridge to the start.

THE PITSTOP

The Old Station Tea Rooms
The excellent breakfasts and cream teas on offer here are a far cry from the 'curly' sandwiches and lukewarm tea of old-school British Rail catering.
Okehampton Station, Station Road, Okehampton EX20 1EJ
Open Wed, Thu & Fri 10–4, Sat & Sun 9–5. 01837 55667
www.dartmoor-railway-sa.org/buffet

THE EXTRA STEP

The military on the moor

Dartmoor's military connections go back more than 200 years, to 1806, when the foundation stone was laid for Dartmoor Prison (see also pp.119 & 126–7), built to house hundreds of French prisoners captured during the Napoleonic Wars. At the same time as building the prison, local MP Sir Thomas Tyrwhitt realised that services and barracks were needed to support it; these barracks were later turned into the Duchy Hotel and now house the High Moors Visitor Centre. Before long, Tyrwhitt's settlement grew to become a small town, Princetown. By 1816, with the wars over and the prisoners repatriated, the prison fell into decline. In 1850, it was transformed into a civilian prison – a role it maintains today, although it now houses mainly non-violent offenders.

But the moor's military connections don't begin and end at the prison – they are far more extensive than that. A permanent British Army training camp and firing range has existed at Okehampton since the 1890s, and, since the beginning of the 20th century, the remoteness of the moor has enabled the Ministry of Defence (MOD) to occupy large swathes of it for training purposes. In 1900, the eccentric vicar of Lewtrenchard, Sabine Baring-Gould, wrote *A Book of Dartmoor*, in which he included military activities among the threats to wilderness on Dartmoor; the other perceived dangers included tin-miners, farmers creating enclosures and the footfall of sightseers. The vicar, in collaboration with Cecil Sharp, the well-known proponent of folk music,

published the song *Widdecombe Fair* in an effort to preserve countryside traditions here. The vicar is also said to have encouraged Arthur Conan Doyle to perpetuate the myth of untamed Dartmoor in his novel *The Hound of the Baskervilles*; the author enjoyed the luxury of the Duchy Hotel when he visited.

The army now controls around a third of Dartmoor, occupying a rough triangle between Okehampton, Lydford and Princetown. Although this is common land and there is public access when the ranges are not in use, army activity still acts as a barrier to those who want to explore the wilder parts of the moor. The aim of the National Park Authority and the Dartmoor Preservation Society is to rid the landscape of live firing and, in 2003, the authority received 1,700 objections to the extension of military use here. Jane Brown sums up this tension between the MOD and the public beautifully in her book *The Everywhere Landscape*, where she describes 'acres of [the moor's] heather scattered with lethal litter'. For Brown, the battle of Dartmoor is between the military, traditional farming practices and public access.

These days, the army promotes the Ten Tors Challenge, a long-distance hike across the moor for teams of young people, including scouts and cadets. It provides thrills, spills and a fair number of accidents each year, especially in poor weather. Many people see the event as a public-relations exercise by the army; others see it simply as an opportunity for local youngsters to explore the beauty and jeopardy of this bewitching landscape.

 152m

 266m

 H

 9km

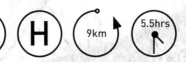 5.5hrs

#1 + 0.5km
#2 + 6km

 #1 - 5.5km
#2 - 2km
#3 - 1.5km

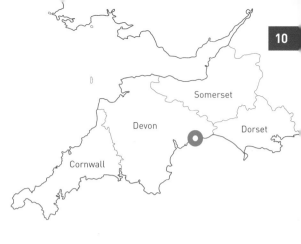

Somerset

Devon

Dorset

Cornwall

Long and taxing but exceptionally beautiful, this walk leads you through a central section of the UNESCO-listed Jurassic Coast and surrounding countryside. Not for the faint-hearted, the route includes several steep climbs, but you'll be amply rewarded for these with jaw-dropping panoramic views from atop the cliffs. The handful of picturesque Pitstops along the route offer plenty of opportunity for a breather, as do a cluster of fascinating National Trust sights in the historic village of Branscombe, including an ancient blacksmith's forge and a restored watermill. Take the utmost care when walking along the dramatic clifftops here, especially on windy days – they are incredibly steep and it's a long way down.

Southleigh

Eppitts

Blackbury
Camp

N

600m
1,500ft

Seaton Road

A3052

Gatcombe Lane

Gabcombe
Coppice

Hollyhead Road

B3174

Locksey's Lane

Stovar Long La

BE

Quarry Lane

Hole
House

Northern Lane

S.#2

Street

Park Road

O.E.#2

Common Hill

Vicarage

Branscombe

S.#1

O.E.#1

Branscombe
Ebb

Branscombe
Beach

Sherborne
Rocks

Beer Head

CLIMBS

150m
125m
100m
75m
50m
25m
0m

1km 2km 3km 4km 5km 6km 7km 8km 9km

GETTING THERE

Following the A3052 in either direction between Sidmouth and Seaton, turn off and follow signs to Branscombe. Park in the car park next to the village hall, which is next to The Forge and near the church. Don't forget to put a donation in the wishing well. EX12 3DA.

WALK DIRECTIONS

1 Come out of the village hall car park, turn left along the lane and, after 50m or so, fork right down a smaller lane, following the public-footpath sign that reads 'Branscombe Mouth & Coastal Path'. At the end of the lane, by the houses and farm, go through the small gate straight ahead onto the surfaced footpath. Follow this, without turning onto smaller paths, all the way to the coast.

2 When you reach the junction with our second Pitstop – the Sea Shanty Beach Café (see p.105) – on your left, turn right onto the pathway signposted West Cliff and Weston Mouth. After the steps near the top of the hill, be sure to enjoy the view along Branscombe beach and on a clear day, far away on the horizon, Chesil Beach and the Isle of Portland. Stay on the main coast path now for about 1km and you will meet a gate. Go left here, signposted Weston Mouth, and walk 150m to a small parking area.

SHORTCUT #1 – About 100m before you reach the gate in Instruction 2, you will see a pathway on the right signposted Branscombe church. This is our first shortcut and will take you back to the church, where you should turn right onto the lane, downhill to the village hall.

3 Back on the main route, at the small parking area, turn right. (Straight ahead is our optional extra, see below.) You will soon find yourself on a clifftop path. Keep going and, after 750m, the path will lead you into a field. Follow the left-hand edge to arrive at a signpost. This is where the optional extra rejoins the route.

OPTIONAL EXTRA #1 – By going straight ahead in the parking area, you'll descend to a secret beach that is featured in our sister publication *Secret Beaches: Southwest England*. It's a long way down and then back up, but worth the effort. Follow the pathway down to sea level, walk along the beach for about 1km and then follow the path back up to the signpost mentioned at the beginning of Instruction 4.

4 At the signpost, turn diagonally back on yourself to the right and cross the field in the direction of the sign points. Walk through a gap in the hedge and across to the far right corner of the next field.

5 From the field corner, turn left onto the lane and walk about 250m to the farm. At the entrance to the caravan park, turn right and then left along the farm lane. After 100m, turn right onto a pathway. Walk along the right-hand field edge, past the back of the farm and into the next field. Follow the arrow left, continuing along the right-hand edge, walk over the hill and finally down a steep pathway to an asphalt lane.

6 Turn left onto the lane towards our first Pitstop, the Fountain Head (see p.105). After 150m (before the pub), turn right onto a slightly concealed pathway. (Even though it runs up the side of a house, rest assured it's public access.) Follow the yellow arrows to the top of the hill and then along the field edges, across the private airfield and onto a narrow lane. Here you can turn right for a shortcut, see below.

SHORTCUT #2 – As mentioned above, for a shortcut here, turn right onto the narrow lane and, avoiding driveways, follow for about 1.5km back down to Branscombe. You will come out at a T-junction. Turn left to walk a final few metres to the start.

7 To continue the route, turn left then immediately right to walk along a public way (which is also an access track for Hole House). You will soon find it turns into a wide path that leads you down the side of a valley to a junction. Turn right and then left onto the lane. Walk past Hole House and then turn onto the pathway on the right (where the lane bends to the left). Follow this down to the bottom of the valley, go over the walkway and stream, and then into the field. Follow the bottom right-hand edge into the next field, then walk diagonally uphill to the far, top, left-hand corner and out onto a lane. Turn right for a shortcut (see below), and left to continue.

SHORTCUT #3 – For this final shortcut, turn right and walk downhill on the lane for about 500m back to Branscombe. You will arrive with the village hall directly next to you on the right.

8 Continue the route by turning left and uphill on the lane. Walk about 100m, then turn right onto the track that cuts backwards to a gate. Go through into the field, walk uphill and over the stile into the next field. Walk diagonally right to the telegraph pole and then veer left to find an overgrown stile into the next field, where you should walk along the left-hand edge to the corner and then into the next field. Here, veer right slightly and walk past the grassy banks on the left, past another telegraph pole and down hill to join a track. Keep following downhill to meet another track, where you should turn left and walk down past the houses to the lane.

9 Turn left on the lane, walk 150m, then turn onto the track on the right, just after a pond. Walk across the shallow stream and follow the track for about 500m. It will turn into asphalt about halfway and lead you to another lane. Turn right (passing the left turn for the second optional extra, see below) and follow downhill into Vicarage village.

10 Arriving in the village, you will see another of our Pitstops, the Masons Arms (see p.105), when the lane bends to the right. But turn left here and then immediately fork right to walk along a narrow lane between houses and alongside a stream. Follow it down to the footbridge, on the other side of which you fork right and follow the surfaced path as it curves right and up the valley. You will recognise this from your outward journey. Follow up to the junction, go straight ahead onto the lane and then, at the T-junction, you will see the start point over to the left.

OPTIONAL EXTRA #2 – This is a long extra and will add a total of 6km to the route. It's a worthy addition for those who want to stretch their legs a bit further than the standard route.

a) At the end of Instruction 9, you turn right onto the lane. Take this turn but instead of walking down into the village, after a few metres of downhill walking, turn left, twice, in quick succession to join a bridleway.

b) Keep following the bridleway by turning left again, to the top of the hill. Follow the left-hand field edge and then go through the gate on the right into the next field.

c) Continue straight and join the main footpath that will lead you to Beer.

d) As you enter Beer, look for pathways and signs that will lead you to the seafront and find your way to the Anchor Inn. With the pub on your right and the sea on your left, walk along the lane that leads past the parking area – you should also see signs marking the coast path.

e) Now follow the coast path in the direction of Branscombe. After about 750m, you pass around Beer Head and you will see the left turn onto the path that leads down to Under Hooken. Take this and follow down to the beach. You'll recognise the Sea Shanty Beach Café ahead of you from Instruction 2 (see p.105). Retrace your steps back up the valley to the start.

NOT TO MISS

The Forge

Branscombe Forge, which dates from 1580, is thought to be the oldest-surviving working thatched forge in Devon. With luck, you'll see the blacksmith at work at the furnace, bending the red-hot metal to create all manner of beautiful ironwork artefacts. The smith here sells his wares direct from the forge.
www.nationaltrust.org.uk/branscombe

The Manor Mill

There used to be four mills in Branscombe, but the only surviving one is this fully restored 19th-century watermill, which is likely to have supplied flour to the Old Bakery at one time. Visitors can learn about the history of the mill through regular demonstrations, and kids can dress up and have a go at turning hand mills.
www.nationaltrust.org.uk/branscombe

The Old Bakery

This beautiful thatched stone building was the last traditional working bakery in the county until its closure in 1987. While enjoying a cup of tea in the café here (see opposite), you'll see some of the original equipment in the baking room, including an old bread oven and proving trough.

THE PITSTOPS

The Fountain Head

This 14th-century pub, which is named after a nearby spring, has an open fire and a flagstone floor. Enjoy the old-fashioned grub and award-winning real ales from the Branscombe Vale Brewery. Branscombe EX12 3BG. Open Mon–Sat 11–3 & 6–11, Sun midday–10.30. 01297 680359 www.fountainheadinn.com

The Sea Shanty Beach Café

Bag an outside table at this charming thatched-roofed café, which is set right on the beach and serves, among other delights, freshly landed crab and ales from a local microbrewery. Branscombe EX12 3DP. Open Easter–Oct daily 8.30–5, Nov–Easter Sat, Sun & bank hols 10–4. 01297 680577. www.theseashanty.co.uk

The Old Bakery

In fine weather, enjoy your cream tea or delicious home-cooked meal in the pretty garden at this National Trust-owned bakery. Branscombe EX12 3DB. Open Easter–May, Sep & Oct daily 10.30–4.30, Jun–Aug daily 10.30–5, Nov–Christmas Sat & Sun 11–4 01752 346585. www.nationaltrust.org.uk/branscombe

The Masons Arms

Another 14th-century inn in this historic village, the Masons Arms serves local Dartmoor produce in its relaxed restaurant, cosy bar and flower-filled garden, which boasts fantastic sea views. Branscombe EX12 3DJ. Open Mon–Sat 11–11, Sun noon–10.30 01297 680300. www.masonsarms.co.uk

THE EXTRA STEP

Mary Anning and the Jurassic Coast

The Jurassic Coast, which runs for 155km from Exmouth in Devon to Swanage in Dorset, is known for its ancient geology, which sheds light on 185 million years of natural history. Over time, the cliffs here have crumbled into the sea, unearthing fossils that reveal the secrets of an impossibly distant past. This UNESCO World Heritage Site attracts both amateur and professional geologists to its fossil-rich beaches, such as Charmouth in Devon. The 10km stretch running from Seaton in Devon to Lyme Regis in Dorset, which lies just to the east of this walk, is famed for its landslips (referred to as 'undercliffs'); the distinctive, white-tipped rock formation on this stretch known as Under Hooken, for example, was formed by a slippage in the chalk cliffs in 1790.

One of the first people to realise the fossil wealth of this remarkable stretch of coastline was the renowned British fossil collector and palaeontologist Mary Anning, who lived in the coastal town of Lyme Regis. From an early age, Mary combed the Jurassic shore, particularly in winter, when landslides gave up their ancient treasures. It was here that she discovered, at the age of 12 and with the help of her brother, a 9m-long skeleton that turned out to be the first correctly identified ichthyosaurus (a large marine reptile from the late Triassic and early Jurassic periods), which now resides in the Natural History Museum in London. Anning also uncovered the remains of the first two plesiosauruses

(marine reptiles) ever found and the first pterosaur (a flying reptile) to have been discovered outside Germany, as well as some important fish fossils.

For Anning, fossil hunting was a perilous passion – in 1833, clambering over the Blue Lias Cliffs, she almost lost her life in the same landslide that killed her dog. But it didn't deter her. And despite the handicaps of both gender and class in a scientific community dominated by well-to-do men, Anning's legacy lives on today, shaping our current view of prehistoric life forms. In spite of her fame, she struggled financially and only received full credit for her discoveries after her death in 1847. In 2010, the Royal Society named her one of the top ten most influential women in the history of British science. Her life is celebrated in a beautiful window in St Michael's Church, Lyme Regis.

More than a century after Anning's death, the English novelist John Fowles set key passages of his 1969 historical work, *The French Lieutenant's Woman*, in the Lyme Undercliff. The protagonist, a serious-minded Victorian gentleman and amateur naturalist named Charles Smithson, falls in love with the unhappy heroine, Sarah Woodruff. By setting the book in Lyme, with its air of primordial mystery, Fowles suggests that there are aspects of the natural world and human relationships that are beyond scientific analysis. Furthermore, this unsettling place disturbs any notions we might have of the earth as a solid, unchanging home. With this message from Fowles in mind, it's vital to keep to marked footpaths on this walk and pay attention to warning signs – despite its great beauty, this area is inherently unstable and full of holes and gullies.

11 Pullabrook Wood
In the footsteps of farmers

201m

211m

E

4.5km

1.5hrs

Somerset

Devon

Dorset

Cornwall

Pullabrook Wood is one of three Woodland Trust-managed sites known collectively as the Bovey Valley Woods, which lie on the eastern edge of Dartmoor, in the lower end of the valley of the River Bovey – an area of international conservation importance. The other two are nearby Hisley and Houndtor woods. This walk, once a well-worn route used by farmers on the way to sell their wares at the market in Bovey Tracey, begins and ends on the historic Drakeford Bridge – a pretty packhorse bridge with unknown beginnings that underwent repairs in 1684, as the tablet set into the side of the parapet testifies. On the way, expect to see lots of wildlife along the sheltered River Bovey – from kingfishers, butterflies and dormice to all kinds of lichens – as well as a diverse array of trees, many of which are ancient. With only two short but steep sections, this route is suitable for walkers of various abilities.

11

Pullabrook Wood

In the footsteps of farmers

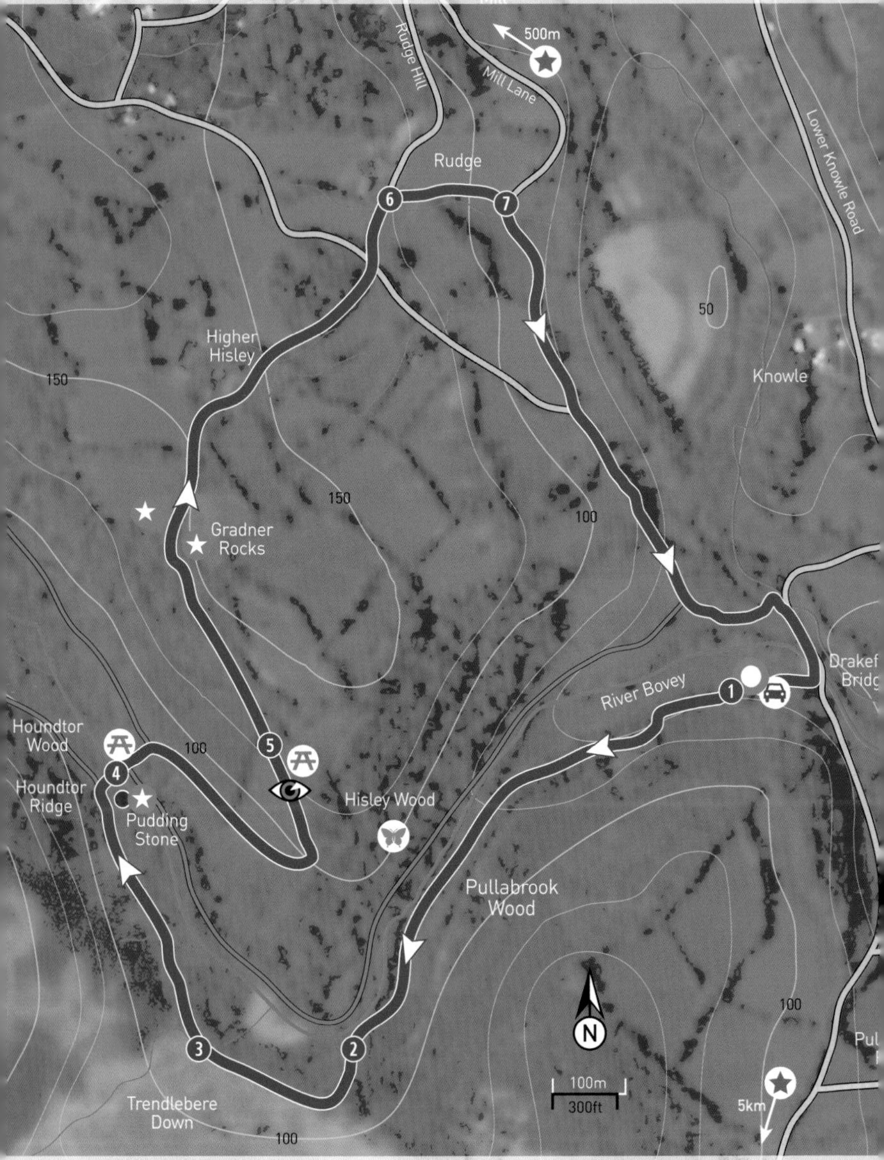

LUSTLEIGH
Wrayland
Mill
500m
Rudge Hill
Mill Lane
Lower Knowle Road
Rudge
6
7
50
Higher Hisley
150
Knowle
150
100
Gradner Rocks
Drakef
Bridg
River Bovey
1
Houndtor Wood
100
5
4
Houndtor Ridge
Pudding Stone
Hisley Wood
Pullabrook Wood
100
N
3
2
Pul
100m
300ft
5km
Trendlebere Down
100

CLIMBS

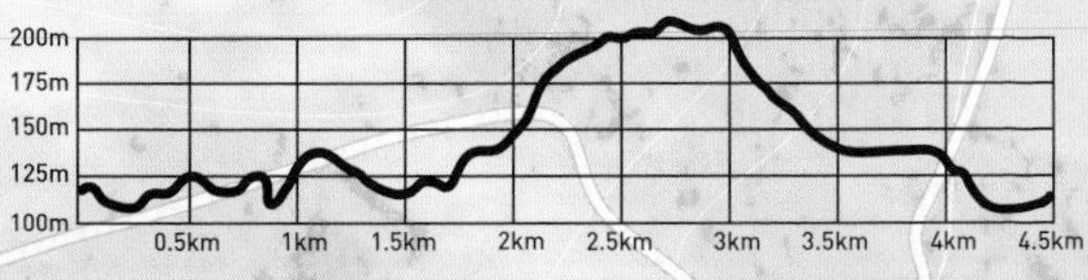

200m
175m
150m
125m
100m
0.5km
1km
1.5km
2km
2.5km
3km
3.5km
4km
4.5km

150

GETTING THERE

Find your way to Lustleigh, drive south onto Mill Lane and follow down the hill to a T-junction, where you should turn right. Drakeford Bridge is just a short distance further, with the car park for the walk start on the other side on the right. TQ13 9LG will take sat-nav users to Pullabrook Farm, which is near Drakeford Bridge.

WALK DIRECTIONS

1 Walk out of the back of the car park onto a wide track. After 200m, turn right onto another track and follow it around to the left. Soon you will be following the River Bovey.

2 Follow the track when it turns up the short, steep hill. Carry straight on at the first junction, turn right at the second and then go through the gate and turn right again. Walk gently downhill now.

3 When you meet a stream, go straight ahead to stay on the same track. The route will level out and, after a few hundred metres, you will see a large, spherical boulder – the Pudding Stone (see below). Turn right at the junction here and go through the gate into Hisley Wood.

NOT TO MISS

The Pudding Stone
In Instruction 3, you'll come to a large, almost perfectly spherical, smooth granite boulder, known as the Pudding Stone. Although its origins and purpose are not known, it's widely believed that this vast rock was rolled down the hill to its current position in ancient times, where it has remained ever since. (SX779799)

4 Cross over a pretty medieval bridge that formed part of the historic trading route. Just here are a couple of peaceful places to stop for a picnic. To continue, turn left after the bridge and walk up the hill for 50m or so to turn right. Walk another 50m or so and fork left to walk uphill again. Outstanding views soon open up over the valley and beyond. Continue along this track as it bends back around to the left. Close by, there is a picnic bench that has the most stunning view.

5 The track soon turns into a pathway and levels out. You will eventually come out at some houses. Follow the signs to the bridleway.

NOT TO MISS

Boulders and rocks

The Bovey Basin lies along the Sticklepath-Lustleigh fault line, which bisects the county of Devon from north to south. In the fields flanking our route, just before you arrive at the houses mentioned in Instruction 5, lie some mysterious rock formations. These are clear indications of the geological volatility of the area in days gone by.

6 At the end of the bridleway, turn right onto the track (a driveway) and continue downhill to the lane.

7 Turn right onto the lane and follow it downhill, ignoring the turning on the left. You will arrive at a T-junction; turn right here and you will soon recognise Drakeford Bridge and the car park where you started.

THE PITSTOPS

The Cleave

This pretty thatched pub, which dates from the 15th century, serves traditional pub food and local ales at reasonable prices. On cold days, the cosy bar, with its roaring open fire, is the place to be, but on warm and sunny days, it has to be the cottage garden.
Lustleigh TQ13 9TJ. Open daily 11–11. 01647 277223
www.thecleavelustleigh.uk.com

The Old Pottery Restaurant

Set on the site of an old pottery within the House of Marbles – a free visitor attraction shining the spotlight on traditional games, puzzles and toys for kids – this restaurant serves everything from traditional English breakfasts to cream teas and cakes to more substantial hot dishes made using local ingredients. Expect plenty of gluten-free options.
House of Marbles, Pottery Road, Bovey Tracey TQ13 9DR
Open Mon–Sat 9–4.50, Sun 10–4.50. 01626 831320
www.houseofmarbles.com

THE EXTRA STEP

Cromwellian connections

Bovey Tracey is a delightful little cob-and granite-built market town that sits on the eastern edge of Dartmoor, giving rise to the slogan 'The Gateway to the Moor' that appears on all its boundary signs. As such, it's a popular jumping-off point for walkers and wildlife enthusiasts heading out onto the moor, with its dramatic tors and stunning array of flora and fauna. But that's not the only reason people are drawn to Bovey Tracey – a place that also boasts a rich and fascinating history, from its Saxon origins to its pivotal role in the English Civil War.

First mentioned in the Domesday Book as Bovi, the town was named Bovitracy in 1309, in honour of the de Tracys, who ruled the area after the Norman Conquest. William de Tracy is said to have been one of the four assassins of Thomas à Becket, the Archbishop of Canterbury, in 1170. His descendant Henry de Tracy, who lived in the Manor House on East Street, created a borough here in the early 13th century – a development that allowed the townspeople to hold a weekly market and an annual three-day fair by the end of the century. Over the years, the town's name has evolved to its current form, Bovey Tracey.

Fast-forward 350 years and the town is in the throes of the English Civil War. Like most of Devon – except Exeter and Barnstaple – it supported the Royalist cause. So much so, in fact, that it took the might of Oliver Cromwell and his Roundhead army to gain control here. First of all, they surprised the Royalist regiments who were playing cards in a house on East Street – legend has it that the Royalists only escaped capture by throwing pennies from the windows to distract the Roundheads, who were notoriously poorly paid. But this diversion tactic was short-lived – the next day, on 9 January 1646, both sides came to blows during the Battle of Bovey Heath, which ended in victory for Cromwell's troops.

Today, there are several reminders in and around the town of Cromwell and this unstable period in history. Bovey Heath, for example, is now a protected ancient site – over the decades, dozens of artefacts from this decisive battle have been unearthed here. There's also the Cromwell Arms on Fore Street and the ruins of an arch just off the main street, dubbed Cromwell's Arch by the locals. Even though this structure was part of a priory and had nothing to do with Cromwell, it serves as a lasting reminder of the community's links to this controversial figure.

558m

506m

H

18.5km

5.5hrs

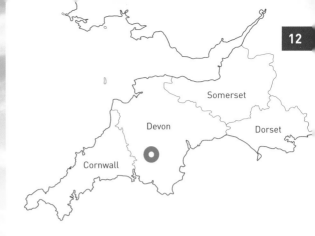

Somerset

Devon

Dorset

Cornwall

You'll need the best part of a day to do justice to this demanding route through west Dartmoor, but fear not – there are two excellent food stops along the way, so you'll be able to rest and refuel at intervals. Prepare to see some fascinating sights as you walk, including historic Dartmoor Prison at Princetown, mysterious Wistman's Wood and two notable tors, with their fabulous countryside views. With boggy patches that become waterlogged after a downpour and several steep sections up and down hills and tors, stout walking shoes are a must. A map and compass are also a sensible idea on such a lengthy walk.

5

1

2

500

400

400

Lydford Tor

400

400

Arch Tor

Longaford
Tor

6

Beardown
Tors

Wistman's
Wood

Chy

5

7 Littaford
Tors

Powdermills

Holming
Beam

400

N

600m
2,000ft

8

Smith Hill

520

B3212

Parson's Cott

Two Bridges 4

B3357

400

3

Prince Hall
Country House 9

HM Prison

PRINCETOWN

1

2

300

300

300

11

Tor Royal

400

10

vil's Bridge

400

400 400

South
Hessary
Tor

400

400

Royal Hill

400

400

But
Circles

400

Cramber Tor

sts

CLIMBS

575m
525m
475m
425m
375m

Pent Col

400

0km 2km 4km 6km 8km 10km 12km 14km 16km 18km

GETTING THERE

Park in the bay just north of Princetown on the B3212 – it's on the left just before the town sign, if you're coming from the Moretonhampstead direction. On the other side of the valley, you will see Dartmoor Prison. PL20 6QU.

WALK DIRECTIONS

1 From the parking bay, turn left onto the road and walk past the Princetown sign. After about 100m, and just after the second house on the left, go through the gate on the left – it is positioned slightly back from the road. This is a public bridleway and easy to follow for about 750m to a T-junction near the bottom of a hill and some farm buildings. Remember this junction (and the way you have come so far) for your return. Turn left here, onto the track, and then go straight ahead onto a pathway when the track bends to the right. Walk about 150m to the two bridges and go over the one on the right to follow alongside the stream for about 500m to the next footbridge.

2 Go over the footbridge and walk straight ahead towards the sparse collection of trees. Go through a gap in a field wall and walk diagonally left and uphill past some large rocks. You should see a footpath sign as you rise up the hill. Walk to this and go through into the next, quite large, field. Here, walk roughly halfway between the two telegraph poles that are in the field ahead of you. You should reach the far boundary at a gate. Go through this and along the path to the road.

3 Turn right onto the road and walk along the wide verge for about 500m to the T-junction after the cattle grid. Turn right and then, after a few metres, fork right to walk over the old bridge just before our first Pitstop, the Two Bridges Hotel (see p.124). In front of the hotel, walk to the left, cross the road and walk through the small parking area to a gate and the start of a track signposted to Wistman's Wood.

4 Joining the track, walk about 750m to a farmhouse. Join the path to the right of the property and, after about 150m, fork left to continue along the side of the valley. Ahead you will see Wistman's Wood and the tors you will be visiting on the top of the hill diagonally to the right.

5 Just before Wistman's Wood (see p.123), you will go through a gate. Left is a route down to the river – an optional detour. Walk straight ahead to explore the wood and then walk along the path on the uppermost (right) edge of the wood. It might be indistinct at times, but it will lead you along to the farthest grouping of trees. Just as you arrive here, turn right onto a small path that will take you directly uphill to Longaford Tor.

NOT TO MISS

Wistman's Wood

This high-altitude wood is tightly packed with twisted dwarf oak trees and moss-covered rocks, which create a distinct air of mystery. In fact, the name Wistman's Wood may well derive from the local word 'wisht', meaning eerie or haunted. The wood is thought to be a remnant of the forest that covered much of the moor in ancient times (see p.126).

THE PITSTOPS

Two Bridges Hotel

This luxury hotel, which was originally an 18th-century coaching inn named The Saracen's Head, has a stylish restaurant serving great-quality, seasonal food that's as superb as the setting. For a small surcharge, pets are given treats and water bowls. Two Bridges, Dartmoor PL20 6SW. Open daily noon–9 01822 892300. www.twobridges.co.uk

Prince Hall Country House

Expect superb food and service in the restaurant of this hotel, beneath which lie the cellars and foundations of a 15th-century mansion that once stood on the site. Dogs are welcome in the bar. Two Bridges, Dartmoor PL20 6SA. Open noon–3 & 7–9 01822 890403. www.princehall.co.uk

6 Arriving at Longaford Tor, be sure to climb one of the rock outcrops where the commanding views of the moor are unmissable. From the top, look south, along the valley from where you have come, and you will see two more tors ahead of you. They are about 250m and 500m away. Walk to the second one, Littaford Tors.

7 As you arrive at Littaford Tor, look diagonally to the left, past the smaller collection of rocks, towards the line of trees and the bottom of the hill. You should be able to make out the grey-slated roof of a building within the trees about 1.5km away. Head directly towards this in a southeasterly direction. Be sure to stay on course as the building will disappear from view for a while. When it comes back into view, follow the stone wall downhill and then left along the bottom edge of the field (with a road on your right) to a stile. Beware of the boggy areas. You will find the stile about 50m after you pass a gate.

8 Go over the stile and cross the road to join a bridleway opposite. Make sure you follow the sometimes indistinct path across this large, open field, roughly in the direction of the buildings in the trees ahead of you. After about 1km, find a safe place to cross the stream and walk uphill to the gate. Go through onto the road and turn right. Walk for 250m and then turn left onto the driveway (and bridleway) leading to our second Pitstop, Prince Hall Country House (see opposite).

9 Arriving at Prince Hall Country House, turn left where signposted and walk on the asphalt track around the house to the opposite side. Then follow the gentle curve to the left, to the old stone bridge. Go over the bridge and through the gate, and follow the track uphill to where it bends sharply to the right. Here, go straight ahead onto the moor once more and follow the bridleway, more or less in a straight line, into a valley and up the other side. Go through a gate halfway up the hill and then, just after the top of the hill, you meet a wide crossways.

10 Turn right and follow the wide bridleway – more like a flattened swathe of grass – for about 750m to a gate and signpost. Turn right towards Princetown and follow another wide bridleway uphill towards the post on the near horizon and slightly to the left of the antenna on the far horizon. When you reach the post, keep going and you will see the rest of the bridleway laid out ahead of you for the next 3km or so.

11 At the end of the bridleway, you reach a house. Go through the gate and walk down the drive. Just after the house, turn right onto a track that runs alongside a stream. About 250m after the house, you arrive at the junction we asked you to remember in Instruction 1. Turn left to walk uphill and follow the bridleway to the road, and then turn right to finish the walk.

THE EXTRA STEP

The people of the moor

The many ancient monuments on Dartmoor bear witness to its long history of human occupation; in fact, more people lived here in prehistoric times than do today. Neolithic and early Bronze Age communities used fire to clear the landscape of forest in order to cultivate crops and establish farming communities, and they mined tin and traded it as far away as the Mediterranean. Today, reminders of these industrious societies lie scattered across the moor in the form of ceremonial granite megaliths. It's said that Dartmoor contains a higher concentration of Bronze Age remains than anywhere else in the country, and although these sites are usually found on the remotest tracts of moor, there are some accessible ruins at Merrivale, a hamlet set in a vast natural amphitheatre about 8km to the west of this walk. The site of a stone circle, a standing stone (or menhir), a double stone row, and the remains of stone tombs (or kistvaens) and round houses, this hamlet paints a vivid picture of what was a complex and highly sophisticated society.

During the first millennium AD, people were forced to abandon the moor due largely to climate change, when longer winters and cooler summers forced communities onto lower ground. In the early medieval period, however, as the climate became warmer again, human occupation re-established itself on the moor, although never in quite such a concentrated way. These later settlers

made use of the landscape's plentiful granite to build sturdy homes in much the same way that their ancestors had. Although many of these longhouses were abandoned, some have survived the centuries and have been adapted for use as farm buildings today.

In later centuries, the bubonic plague was rampant here, with 575 deaths in nearby Tavistock alone. In 1625, Merrivale was used as a Plague Market, or Potato Market – a place where the survivors of unfortunate Tavistock could come to trade. According to tradition, coins for payment were left in jars filled with vinegar, which was believed to be an antiseptic. It has also been suggested that Merrivale was used as a vast rabbit warren from medieval times to the mid-19th century, for the breeding of rabbits for meat and fur.

Near to both Wistman's Wood and Merrivale lies Dartmoor Prison, which, in 1809, became home to 2,500 French prisoners from the Napoleonic Wars (see also pp.94–5 & 119). By 1812, American POWs had arrived from the War of 1812 – often considered an extension of the Napoleonic Wars – and there were an astonishing 9,000 inmates here, living in dreadful conditions. When the wars ended in 1815 and the prisoners were repatriated, the prison fell into decline. It wasn't until the middle of the 19th century that it became a custodial prison – a role it maintains today, although it now houses mainly white-collar offenders. From the stone circle at Merrivale, it's still possible to make out the track of the old Princetown railway, which once carried granite from the moor and prospective inmates up to the gaol at Princetown.

 522m

 358m

 H

 11km

4hrs

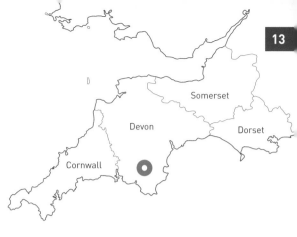

Somerset

Devon

Dorset

Cornwall

Only an intrepid few are prepared to explore such demanding tracks off the normal dog-walkers' route, but the magnificent views and fragments of ancient history along the way are worth every step. It's imperative that you take a map and compass with you on this journey, which involves several indistinct paths and steep sections. The ground can get a little boggy in parts, so wear appropriate footwear, as well as gaiters or waterproof trousers in the wetter seasons, when the area's copious bracken holds a great deal of moisture. This walk is not recommended on rainy or foggy days, but is lovely in fine weather, when the far-reaching views from the top of Eastern White Barrow are truly breathtaking.

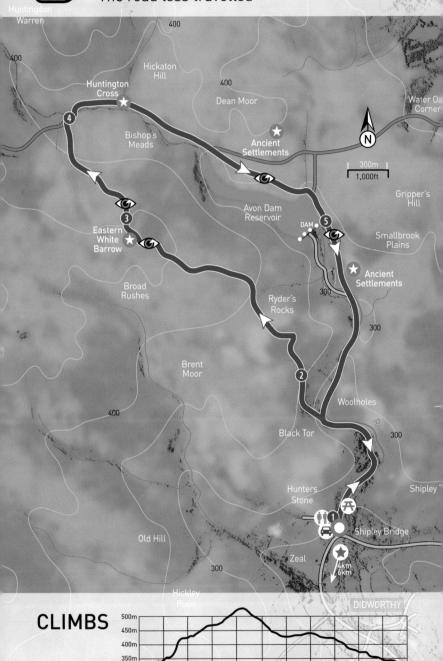

Huntingdon
Warren

400

Hickaton
Hill

400

Huntington
Cross ⭐

Dean Moor

Water Oak
Corner

4

Bishop's
Meads

⭐
Ancient
Settlements

N

300m
1,000ft

Gripper's
Hill

3

Avon Dam
Reservoir

DAM 5

Smallbrook
Plains

⭐
Eastern
White
Barrow

⭐ Ancient
Settlements

300

Broad
Rushes

Ryder's
Rocks

300

Brent
Moor

2

400

Woolholes

300

Black Tor

River

300

Hunters
Stone

Shipley

1

Shipley Bridge

Old Hill

Zeal

⭐
4km
6km

Hickley
Plain

300

DIDWORTHY

CLIMBS

500m
450m
400m
350m
300m

0km 1km 2km 3km 4km 5km 6km 7km 8km 9km 10km 11km

Brent Fore
Hill

Badworthy

GETTING THERE

Shipley Bridge (SX68162) is north of South Brent and Didworthy, just off the A38. The postcode TQ10 9EL will take a sat-nav device into Didworthy. Any good map will show how to find Shipley Bridge from Didworthy. The large car park is just next to the bridge.

WALK DIRECTIONS

1 From the car park, walk to the bridge and turn left up the asphalt bridleway. You will be walking upstream with the river on your right. After 250m, ignore the left turn at the junction and keep going for about another 750m to a small bridge. Do not go over the bridge; instead, go straight ahead onto a pathway beside the river, which may be boggy. After 100m, turn up the hill, where you see a way up. Now walk northwest up the steep incline. You will be heading roughly in the direction of a solitary tree about two thirds of the way up. (The pathway here is, at best, indistinct. And in summer you may find yourself trailblazing through bracken.)

2 Upon reaching the top of the hill, you will see Eastern White Barrow silhouetted on the horizon ahead of you. It is on the top of a hill. Head straight for it, into a shallow valley at first and then uphill for 2km or so.

NOT TO MISS
Eastern White Barrow
This impressive stone structure – a heap of granite with a circular tower at its centre – is a Bronze Age cairn and burial site. Its location on the crest of a hill and its commanding size imply that whoever was buried here was considered extremely important. On clear days, the views from this point are astonishing. (SX665652)

3 After the barrow, keep going on a northwest bearing, roughly towards the stream running down the valley ahead of you (there is also a tall communications mast on a distant hill slightly to the left). You will descend into a valley – it's not particularly steep, but watch out for small dips between the grass tufts, and boggy areas.

4 You will eventually arrive at the bank of the River Avon, where it is still quite small. Look for the ford near to where you arrive. If you can't find it, it might mean that the water is too high – in this case, find a safe place to cross using stepping stones. Safely on the opposite bank, turn right and you should pick up an indistinct path next to the river. After a couple of hundred metres, you reach a fence and a stone cross (see below). Keep going and the path will become more distinct and eventually lead you past the reservoir.

NOT TO MISS

Ancient settlements
These are very clear to make out from where you stand on Eastern White Barrow in Instruction 2, and you will see more as you walk towards the reservoir. Their shapes and sizes vary greatly – one is almost heart-shaped. (SX660657)

NOT TO MISS

Huntington Cross
Originally a waymarker on the Abbots' Way – a track for monks travelling between monasteries in medieval times – this cross was used in the mid-16th century by Sir William Petre as one of four to mark the boundary of his manor. (SX660657)

5 Arriving at the dam, keep going and the path turns into a track. The Avon Dam was built in 1957 and holds back 1.3 billion litres of water, weighing an impressive 1.3 million tons, which feeds into the South Hams water system. At the end of the track, you meet an asphalt lane. This is the asphalt bridleway you walked up at the beginning of the route. Turn left and follow it for 3km back to the start.

THE PITSTOPS

Turtley Corn Mill

The food served in this ivy-clad mill building, which is located 6km away on the other side of the A38, is locally sourced – in fact, the eggs come from the chickens that roam the grounds alongside guinea fowl, ducks and peacocks. Avonwick, South Brent TQ10 9ES. Open Mon–Sat 8.30–11, Sun 8.30–10.30. 01364 646100. www.turtleycornmill.com

The Oak

This locals' favourite, which is slightly closer than Turtley Corn Mill, serves real ale and traditional pub food, which is freshly made and locally sourced. Station Road, South Brent TQ10 9BE. Open Mon & Tue 4–11, Wed & Thu noon–2 & 4–11, Fri noon–2 & 4–midnight, Sat noon–midnight, Sun noon–10.30. 01364 72133. www.oakonline.net

THE EXTRA STEP

The story of the Dartington Estate

The sprawling, splendid Dartington Estate, which lies roughly 14km to the east of this walk, is an ancient country pile that's been a hub of industry and the arts for more than 90 years. Its long-standing reputation as a powerhouse of rural regeneration is the work of Leonard and Dorothy Elmhirst, who bought the derelict medieval estate in 1925 – when the local agricultural community was at its most depressed and impoverished between the wars – and set about restoring it in a way that would benefit the local community.

The pioneering couple were inspired by the work of the Indian Nobel laureate Rabindranath Tagore, who had introduced progressive education and rural development to the small town of Santiniketan in India. Leonard met Tagore in the United States in the early 1920s and, struck by his vision for the reconstruction of rural communities, travelled to India to help him in his endeavours, setting up an Institute of Rural Reconstruction very near to Santiniketan. It was Tagore who encouraged Leonard to buy and rejuvenate Dartington, using Santiniketan as his model.

And so this estate in the heart of rural Devon became a cultural, educational and economic hub. It was the site of musical and theatrical productions and schools of arts and crafts, as well as the beautiful pottery of Bernard Leach, who worked and taught here. It was also the home of Dartington Hall School, which was founded in the 1930s and rapidly acquired an international reputation as a progressive school nurturing the individual needs and talents of its pupils. Although the school closed amid scandal in 1987 – a victim of its own progressiveness – the lovingly restored medieval Great Hall is now open to visitors.

Dartington is also known for having been a place of agricultural innovation and industry, from weaving to forestry. Not all of Leonard's methods in this area would be regarded as sustainable by current standards – for example, he kept battery hens and cut down hedges to increase field size – but his attitude to forestry, in particular, which involved processing local timber at an on-site sawmill and using it as a building material on the estate, was unmistakably forward-thinking.

In 1935, the Elmhirsts established the Dartington Hall Trust, a registered charity, which continues to run the estate and its yearly programme of concerts, theatre, films and festivals today.

 117m

 340m

 H

 12km

4hrs

Somerset

Devon

Dorset

Cornwall

It may have a fairly heavy-going coastal stretch in the middle, but this walk offers a section towards the end with a level of peace and tranquillity that more than makes up for any physical exertion along the way. The route runs along quiet country lanes to the beautiful, sheltered Wonwell beach to the picture-perfect village of Ringmore, known for its historic pub, the Journey's End Inn. Except this is not quite the end of your journey; instead, you continue on across lovely, open countryside and descend into and climb out of a valley as you head back to the start, where, happily, another pub awaits you. This is a walk with huge appeal – especially when you factor in the majestic sea views from high up on the coast-path stretch.

MODBURY

Goutsford Br

Jubilee Bridge

Little Orcheton

Butland

Ashridge

Little Modbury

Holbeton

Hunts Cross

100

Oldaport

Wastor Cross

Seven Stone Cross

Clyng Mill

100

Lower Torr

Langston Cross

Torr Down

Blackpost Cross

South Langston

KINGSTON

Mothecombe

100

2

Malthouse Point

Wonwell Beach

3

Marwell Cross

1

8

Okenbury

7

Marwell

100

Erme Mouth

Muxham Point

Scobbiscombe Farm

100

6

5

100

Westcombe Beach

4

Ringmore

Ayrmer Cove

Challaborough

BIGBURY-ON SEA

N

600m
2,000ft

Bigbury Bay

Folly hill

CLIMBS

100m
75m
50m
25m
0m

2km 4km 6km 8km 10km 12km

GETTING THERE

Kingston is just south of Modbury in the South Hams district of Devon. Make you way to the village centre and there are two areas to park: the first is next to the church and the Dolphin Inn; the other is just near it on the other side of the pub garden. TQ7 4QE.

WALK DIRECTIONS

1 With your back to the front door of the Dolphin Inn, turn right, walk to the T-junction and then turn right again. Walk up the hill for about 100m to the thatched house and turn right onto the narrow lane directly opposite. At the crossroads, go straight on, signposted Wonwell beach, and then go left after about 700m at another crossroads. This lane will take you down to Wonwell beach.

2 Arriving at Wonwell beach, the lane will end at a wide pathway, at the end of which you will see the beach.

LOW-TIDE ROUTE – Walk straight ahead and down onto the sand. Follow the left-hand side of the estuary around to a wider stretch of sand, where you will see where to join the coast path near a stream.

HIGH-TIDE ROUTE – Just where the lane turns into a wide pathway, turn left onto the path signposted Bigbury-On-Sea. Follow this to the next section of beach where, just after the stream, the low- and high-tide options join up with each other again.

3 Now simply follow the coast path for about 3.5km. After 3km, you will come across the first footbridge at Westcombe beach. Keep going here, over the next headland, to Ayrmer Cove, where you meet the second footbridge. Go over the bridge and turn left after about 50m, onto the long, straight pathway heading inland. When you meet the gate, go straight ahead instead of right to the car park. After about 150m, you will arrive at a lane.

4 Turn right onto the lane and walk 150m to the T-junction. Turn left and walk downhill, veering right past our Pitstop, the Journey's End Inn (see p.143). At the next junction, go straight ahead uphill and past the church. Just after the church, turn left onto a lane and walk around the back of the graveyard.

5 After 150m on this lane, turn left onto the pathway just after a house called The Manor. Follow the yellow arrows through the fields and down into the valley. Be careful not to miss one of the turnings as you approach the valley.

6 Before the valley bottom, you go over a stream and join a track heading downhill. When you arrive at a second stream and a derelict house, go over the stream and along the edge of the field with the stream just to your right. Keep going to the end of the field and join the path into the woods. Just before you exit the woods, the path takes you straight up a steep hill for about 150m.

7 At the top of the hill, turn right and walk along two sides of the field (don't cross over into the next field) to a track. Turn right and then, just after the first bend, turn right onto a pathway that leads directly across a field to a lane. Turn left onto the lane and, after 50m, turn right to rejoin a pathway. Now follow the arrows again all the way back to Kingston.

8 You will come out at a lane next to a house. Turn right to walk uphill to a T-junction. Turn right here, walk downhill and you will see the pub up the first road on the left.

THE PITSTOP

The Journey's End Inn
This 13th-century free house manages to tread a fine line between cosy locals' favourite and thriving gastro-pub. Four open fires roar continuously throughout the winter, while in summer, the large beer garden fills up fast. Dogs are welcome in all areas of the pub. Ringmore, Kingsbridge TQ7 4HL. Open Tue–Fri noon–3 & 6–11, Sat & Sun noon–11. 01548 810205. www.thejourneysendinn.co.uk

THE EXTRA STEP

The South Hams coast path

The South Hams, a lovely area of rural and coastal Devon, includes one of the most unspoilt stretches of the South West Coast Path, running from Plymouth in the west to Torbay in the east. But this is also one of the most challenging sections, with large rivers and sprawling estuaries to negotiate en route.

From Plymouth's historic Barbican area – one of the few parts of the city to have escaped destruction in World War II – a ferry runs all year across to Mount Batten Park in the east, known for its watersports centre. Along the coast from here, you'll find a beach at Wembury that offers great rock-pooling, swimming, surfing and kayaking, as well as a popular café. But it's on the next stretch of coast, beyond the River Yealm, that the fun really begins. Cross the river-mouth by ferry here – check the tide-dependent times in advance – and head for the quaint village of Noss Mayo on the other side. The pubs on Newton Creek, a tributary of the Yealm Estuary, are a big draw for twitchers and artists, who come to admire both migratory birds and native species.

The next river along, the Erme, is altogether more challenging. Intrepid walkers who wish to cross the mouth of the river, instead of taking a 13km trek inland, need to plan well ahead. The river can be forded, but only during an hour-long period on either side of low tide. Timetable-information

boards advising walkers of the safest route across can be found on both the Mothercombe bank, near the old coastguard cottages, and on the Wonwell bank, near the slipway. Time it right, and the water should be no higher than knee-deep. For obvious reasons, this route is safer in summer than in winter.

The next hurdle is distinctive Burgh Island, just offshore. This craggy outcrop is home to the white Art Deco Burgh Island Hotel, built in 1929. Visited by the English playwright and wit Noel Coward, the hotel gained great popularity in the 1930s with sophisticated holidaymakers and still oozes glamour today. At the other end of the scale and yet part of the same establishment is the 700-year-old Pilchard Inn, originally frequented by fishermen and smugglers. The island can be accessed at any time of day, either on foot at low tide or by sea tractor at high tide. Beyond, the estuary of the Avon might look like an easy walk at low tide, but the main channel here is deep and fast-flowing at all times. A ferry runs in the morning and afternoon throughout the summer.

Further east lies the sprawling Kingsbridge estuary, with its finger-like inlets and creeks, where a year-round ferry runs from the classy resort of Salcombe to the small village of East Portlemouth on the eastern side. The final crossing to make along this route is over the wide mouth of the River Dart, on the ferry from Dartmouth to Kingswear. If you're here in the summer and happen to stumble upon either Salcombe or Dartmouth regatta week, prepare to be wowed – the sight of hundreds of boats on the water, from tall ships to gigs, is nothing short of magical.

 133m

 248m

M/H

13km

4.5hrs

+5km

#1 - 6km
#2 - 4km

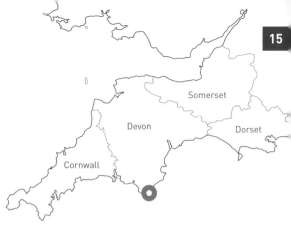

Somerset

Devon

Dorset

Cornwall

This is a spectacular walk along one of the most impressive sections of the South West Coast Path, including Prawle Point – the most southerly point in Devon. It's a good idea to take a basket or bag with you, if your visit coincides with summer berry season, when these fruits, ripe for the picking, spring up in abundance in the hedgerows that line the route. It might be quite long and a little uneven in places, but this walk only has one big and steep climb and has plenty of shortcuts. Highlights include a wrecked cargo ship, a lighthouse, the perfect pub for a slap-up meal and no less than five secret beaches – the reason why we featured this area in our other book *Secret Beaches: Southwest England*. If you'd like to extend the walk we've given you instructions to make an impressive 18km hike. If you do this, be sure to carry plenty of water with you, as there's nowhere en route to stop for refreshments.

15 Prawle Point
Harvesting hedgerows in South Devon

CLIMBS

GETTING THERE

East Prawle is a small village at the very southern tip of the South Hams district in Devon. It's a few miles east of Salcombe. Find your way to the village green, where there is a small parking area. TQ7 2BY.

WALK DIRECTIONS

1 Standing on the road next to the parking area at the village green, orientate yourself so that the public conveniences are on your right and the café is across the green on your left. Walk ahead down the lane, away from the village and towards the coast. When the road bends sharply to the left after 400m, go straight ahead onto a bridleway and walk about 300m to a junction. Turn left onto the pathway downhill.

2 This takes you to the coast path, where you should turn right and then left to follow the lower route. Keep following this up and over the steep part to arrive at Prawle Point after about 1.5km – the sea will be on your right.

SECRET BEACH #1 – Just after turning right and then left in Instruction 2, you'll see a wooden post. This marks a steep descent to our first secret beach on this walk, known locally as Macely beach.
SECRET BEACH #2 – 250m after turning right and then left in Instruction 2, you'll arrive at a gate. Just after this is an even steeper and more vertiginous descent to Elender Cove, a sandy haven like Macely.

3 Keep going on the coast path after Prawle Point for about 2km and you will reach two gates. Go through them and follow the right-hand field border all the way around to a junction. At this point, left is our first shortcut and right is the continuation of the route.

SECRET BEACH #3 – Landing Cove is about halfway between Prawle Point and the junction mentioned in Instruction 3. It is a small beach of wide, flat pebbles that has a low (safe) cliff on its northerly side. With it's south-facing position and part of the beach accessible at high tide, it is a good place to stop for a picnic if there's a brisk northerly blowing. Look for small off-shoot pathways down the low cliff to the beach.
SHORTCUT #1 – This will cut our route to about 7km in total, and it's only 1km back to the start from where you join the shortcut. Although the route is steep in parts, it's easy to find your way to the village (you need to turn right twice for the quickest route back).

4 Back on the route, there's a relatively flat section for about 1km before you arrive at a junction. Turn right to the beach or left to walk around the house. Just after the stream on this section is our second shortcut.

SECRET BEACH #4 – Woodcombe Sand is a sandy haven, little visited even in summer. Take time to enjoy the tranquillity before heading off.

SHORTCUT #2 – This will cut our route to about 9km; it's about 2km back to the start from where you join the shortcut. Follow the path about 500m up to a junction and then pick up from Instruction 9 by turning left.

5 Back on the coast path after Woodcombe Sand, you will arrive at another point where you walk around a house. Again, here, you have the option to visit a secret beach.

SECRET BEACH #5 – Signposted from the coast path is Ivy Cove, another sandy slip of joy, secluded and unknown to many.

6 Finally, the coast path brings you to Lannacombe Cove, which is our recommended picnic spot as it's at the end of the route on the coast path and about halfway along our route. After enjoying the beach, head inland on the narrow lane for about 750m. You arrive at a T-junction. Turn left and then left again (signposted S. Allington and Chivelstone) to follow another narrow lane downhill and past some houses.

OPTIONAL EXTRA – If you have the time and are enjoying the coastal views, then continue on the coast path all the way to Start Point and the lighthouse – extending the route to a total of 18km. This is a slightly arduous stretch, but you will be rewarded with a beach featured in *Secret Beaches: Southwest England* – Great Mattiscombe Sand – and, upon arriving at the lighthouse, views that extend further along the coast to the northeast, towards Dartmouth. After the lighthouse, walk to the car park and follow the lane inland past the farm. After about 1.5km, at the crossroads turn left onto another lane and follow to the next junction. Turn left at this junction and walk downhill past the houses. Pick up from Instruction 7 by turning left onto the bridleway signposted E. Prawle.

7 About 100m after the houses and a short uphill section, turn left onto the bridleway signposted E. Prawle. Follow uphill on the zigzags to the right and, when the path opens up to a field, walk directly up the steep hill to the uppermost left-hand corner. (In summer, you may be walking along an indistinct path through bracken.) In the next field, follow the right-hand edge to the gate and go through onto the track.

8 You are now on a bridleway. Go through gates and follow the arrows which, after about 1km, will take you around the back of a farm. Keep going on the bridleway to about 500m after the farm, where the route dips into a small valley. After this, make sure you take the right turn past the large pond and across the field on the diverted route. After the field, go through the two gates and you will see a path on the left – this is where our second shortcut joins the route.

9 Walk straight past the point at which the shortcut joins the route and soon you'll meet a lane at a bend. Turn right (straight ahead) and follow this to the second sharp bend, then rejoin the bridleway on the left. Follow this all the way to another lane on the outskirts of East Prawle. (Make sure you take the right turn after 500m or so – look for the blue arrow.)

10 Turn left onto the lane and follow it down the hill and around bends into East Prawle. Follow the lane back up the hill on the other side, turning left at the T-junction and then right to continue uphill past our Pitstop, the Pigs Nose Inn (see below), and back to the start at the village green.

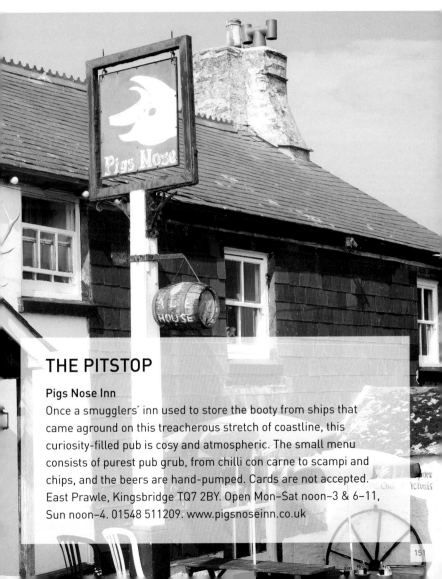

THE PITSTOP

Pigs Nose Inn

Once a smugglers' inn used to store the booty from ships that came aground on this treacherous stretch of coastline, this curiosity-filled pub is cosy and atmospheric. The small menu consists of purest pub grub, from chilli con carne to scampi and chips, and the beers are hand-pumped. Cards are not accepted. East Prawle, Kingsbridge TQ7 2BY. Open Mon–Sat noon–3 & 6–11, Sun noon–4. 01548 511209. www.pigsnoseinn.co.uk

THE EXTRA STEP

Slapton Sands – the Americans in Devon

It took local resident Ken Small many years to uncover the mystery of the Americans at Slapton Sands revealed in his book, *The Forgotten Dead*. Today, a granite obelisk on the beach, midway between Strete Gate and Torcross, recounts how, in the final weeks of 1943, 3,000 local people were evacuated from local villages at very short notice. This upheaval enabled the US Army to use Slapton Sands for a large-scale rehearsal in preparation for the Normandy landings of 1944. One of a series of 'secret manoeuvres' orchestrated by the Allies ahead of the D-Day landings, Exercise Tiger, on 28 April 1944, turned out to be a disaster, resulting in the deaths of nearly 1,000 US servicemen.

Slapton Sands, with its distinctive shingle bank separating a freshwater lake from the sea, was chosen as the training ground for this ill-fated exercise because of its similarities to Utah beach in northern France, the westernmost of the five landing beaches identified by the Allies. The practice assault at Slapton Sands involved 30,000 troops, nine landing ships and live firing, but when communication broke down, many troops died in friendly fire. Soon afterwards, nine German E-boats attacked a separate convoy of troops making its way for a mock landing at Slapton Sands from Lyme Bay, killing 749 Americans.

At the time, in the run-up to the invasion of Normandy, the tragedy was kept under wraps. Sadly, however, it remained 'forgotten' for many decades after the war, perhaps due to official embarrassment about what had happened or because events had been buried for so long by then already. It wasn't until Ken Small's book was published, 40 years later, that the world really knew what happened at Slapton Sands during that fateful week in 1944. It had taken the Devon resident years to uncover and piece together this fascinating story, through first-hand accounts, including interviews with eyewitnesses. Helped more by local residents than by either the US or British armies, he also organised the recovery of a wreck of a Sherman tank and preserved it as a memorial to the men who lost their lives. The tank can be seen today, at the entrance to the village of Torcross, at the southern end of Slapton Sands.

In 1987, Ken Small's efforts were at last rewarded by the United States Secretary of Defense, who dedicated a plaque at the site of the tank to those who lost their lives. These days, the descendants of the heroes of this event leave messages of remembrance taped to the hulk of the tank. Similar acts of thanksgiving take place at other memorials, at Utah beach in Normandy, France, and at two sites in the United States: New Bedford, Massachusetts, and Mexico, Missouri. And it's all down to the extraordinary tenacity of local resident Ken Small, who sought justice for the men who died here after finding evidence of the catastrophe washed up on the beach in the 1970s.

BEST WALKS FOR...

...SUNSETS

D.03 Clovelly & Mouthmill
D.04 Roborough
D.08 Roadford Lake
D.14 The Erme Estuary

...LONG HIKES

D.01 Heddon Valley
D.10 Branscombe
D.07 Cadeleigh & Bickleigh
D.15 Prawle Point (optional extra)

...NATURE

D.03 Clovelly & Mouthmill
D.06 Stoodleigh & Oakford
D.10 Branscombe
D.12 Dartmoor Tors & Wistman's Wood

...SWIMMING & SUNBATHING

D.09 Okehampton Station
D.11 Pullabrook Wood
D.10 Branscombe
D.15 Prawle Point

...BREATHTAKING VIEWS

D.01 Heddon Valley
D.03 Clovelly & Mouthmill
D.12 Dartmoor Tors & Wistman's Wood
D.13 Brent Moor & the Avon Dam

...FAMILIES

D.05 Molland & Anstey Gate
D.07 Cadeleigh & Bickleigh (Shortcut #1)
D.09 Okehampton Station
D.10 Branscombe (Shortcut #1)

...PITSTOPS

D.04 Roborough
D.07 Cadeleigh & Bickleigh
D.13 Brent Moor & the Avon Dam
D.15 Prawle Point

...CHALLENGING HILLS

D.01 Heddon Valley
D.07 Cadeleigh & Bickleigh
D.14 The Erme Estuary
D.15 Prawle Point (optional extra)

ABOUT THE AUTHOR

Rob Smith, founder of the *Secret Seeker* guidebook series, has always had a love of walking which stems from long summer holidays spent in southwest England as a child. In his late teens, he moved to France to follow his passion for cooking, working his way up from *plongeur* to chef at a variety of restaurants. He travelled leisurely from Provence to Paris before returning to the UK in 1996 to establish *The Shoreditch Map*. This monthly listings magazine, for which he wrote about venues and events across the stylish London neighbourhood, ran for over 80 issues before he passed it on as a successful enterprise.

These days Rob divides his time between London and Ibiza, where he works on book production and design, delegating the field work to researchers, editors, photographers and writers. Travelling to research locations to check the work of researchers and writers is a welcome break from the office-based work on production.

Rob hopes that his fledgling publishing company will grow and the books he publishes will gain a keen following of users who appreciate handpicked and carefully researched content, as well as good design and evocative writing. Keep your eye on secretseeker.com for more books in the series.

ACKNOWLEDGEMENTS

As well as the kind help and hospitality of the people of Devon, Rob would like to pass on his profound gratitude to the following people.

Katie Halpin and Alex Whittleton, faultless editors who worked tirelessly on the words and content. Steve Marvell and John Payne for their excellent contributions to the research and the Extra Step articles, respectively. Ben Hoo and Nicola Erdpresser – Ben for the overall design and Nicola for the solid desktop publishing. Brendan Barry for the outstanding and inspiring photography. And finally Jo Kirby and Becky Fountain for guidance, advice, proofing and much-needed support.